A Modest Manual
for Living on Earth

A Modest Manual for Living on Earth

Charles Albert Marks

Epigraph Books
Rhinebeck, New York

ISBN: 978-1-948796-16-3

Library of Congress Control Number: 2018944244

Book design by Colin Rolfe
Cover art by Jessica Jones

Epigraph Books
22 East Market Street, Suite 304
Rhinebeck, NY 12572
(845) 876-4861
www.epigraphPS.com

For my mother

Table of Contents

Preface   IX

Introduction   XIII

1. Eternity   1

2. Divinity   12

3. Unity   22

4. Duality   28

5. You Choose Your Thoughts   45

6. Coming Here on Purpose   56

7. The Truth Always Outs   63

8. The Cyclical Nature of Physical Reality   73

9. Having It Made   80

10. Vibrations   86

11. Plenty of Everything for Everybody   101

12. Pain   107

13. Positive and Negative Motivation   118

14. Action Is Its Own Reward   125

15. The Perfection of Each Moment   131

16. The Work Will Always Be Here   136

17. Action and Rest   143

18. Death   149

19. Death (continued)   156

20. Reincarnation and Karma   164

21. Money   176

22. We Are All Bait   180

23. Evil   185

24. Being Tested, and Encountering New Tests   193

25. Unconditional Love   199

26. Acknowledging One's Worthiness   206

27. The Empty Soul   217

28. Epilogue   226

Preface

Can it be said, for each one of us, that the sum of our lifetime's activities and experiences will fulfill a purpose? My answer, which was not arrived at quickly or easily, is yes. Even though most of us will lead pretty humble lives, and our everyday actions will play no crucial role in influencing the direction of history or society, we each have a purpose in this life. We all come to this world, as it were, on assignment.

I began this life, as I'm sure many do, brimming with dreams and plans. When I became an adult, and entered the workaday world, I encountered obstacles—many obstacles—that I had not anticipated when I was sketching out all my lofty goals. These obstacles thwarted many of my plans, and in doing so they performed the very important function of revealing to me the essential tasks I had come here to perform. In my youthful, enthusiastic dreams of the great life I would lead, I compiled a long list of fine and noble achievements I wished to attain. The only problem is that it would have taken several centuries to accomplish everything I had put on my "to do" list.

The obstacles and setbacks we encounter force us to make decisions, to go back to our lists and cross off those entries that, while commendable, are not aligned with the deepest stirrings of our heart and soul. We can all make long lists of things we would like to do, given enough time, materials, training, money, etc. But then there are certain things that we MUST do, are driven to do regardless of lacking the time, money, and other seemingly necessary resources. These comprise our purpose in life. Literally, it is what we came into this life to do. Each one of us has a unique purpose, which is determined by what we have chosen to learn and experience in this lifetime. For one person, it may be to work as a short-order cook. For another, it may be bearing and raising six children. Another person's purpose might be to engage in the great debates of the day, spend decades in elective office, run for President of the United States, and lose.

One purpose of my life was to write this book, even though as recently as four years ago, I had no inkling that I would write in this manner. From an early age, I aspired to be a writer, but I was most interested in writing fiction—novels, short stories, and screenplays. However, life has its own ways of guiding us to certain paths and revealing our proper tasks to us.

A peculiar biographical fact of my life is that I attained one of my greatest desires at the tender age of twenty-five. A storybook mansion had captured my imagination. It was on an estate not far from where I grew up, and I wanted to own it. Thinking along conventional lines, I figured I would go out into the world, make a fortune, and buy the place. However, my youthful attempts to become a great success in business resulted in multiple financial setbacks. Then, right at the lowest ebb of my material fortunes, I moved into the mansion of my dreams. Not as the owner, but as the caretaker!

The ensuing years on this property presented me with a unique set of opportunities. The estate was scenic and secluded, surrounded by hundreds of acres of unspoiled forest. There was plenty of challenging outdoor work to do, which I enjoyed. More importantly, it was an ideal place in which I could pursue my deeper interests—reading, studying, contemplating, and writing. In addition, this property was within an hour's drive of a major metropolitan center, which enabled me to attend many stimulating lectures, seminars, and conferences. The combination of my exposure to first-rate thinkers and teachers, on one hand, and solitary time in a peaceful setting where I could reflect and ruminate, on the other hand, led to the development and articulation of the insights presented in this book.

I make no claim to have invented or discovered the precepts offered here. Most of these insights have been known, written about, and taught for thousands of years. However, although I learned and memorized many of them in school, I didn't truly KNOW any of them. When we encounter a truth mentally, we do so in a detached way. One of the essential purposes of living in this world is to translate our mental and spiritual understanding into concrete action.

Because I was largely isolated from the constant chatter and stress that most people experience every day, I had the opportunity to explore and probe these insights. By contemplating and reflecting on each one of these concepts, I tested its validity and verified it in terms of my own life. Then I proceeded to apply and incorporate each insight into the daily workings of my life. By consistently acting in accordance with each precept, I transformed them from abstract concepts into intrinsic aspects of my character. Instead of being merely ideas to think and talk about, they became inalienable parts of my being. At this point it became my duty to communicate what I had learned to others; hence this book.

Throughout the ages, humans have spent most of their time and attention looking after physical needs and desires. Rarely, and usually only during times of trauma or loss, do we inquire into the deeper meanings of why we decided to engage in a physical experience in the first place. As I mentioned above, most of the insights presented here have been a part of our spiritual legacy for thousands of years. Unlike inherited physical traits such as eye color, however, they are lessons that each individual must learn and realize for himself or herself.

It may be necessary to rewrite these lessons each generation or so, since the use of words and language is ever changing and evolving. In this way, the teachings will remain fresh, accessible, and comprehensible. And that has been my purpose: to translate these insights into the idiom of our present age.

Introduction

Imagine that interplanetary travel has become commonplace. You can book a vacation on Mars or one of the moons of Jupiter as easily as going to Hawaii or the Bahamas. However, each planet has a distinct environment, which is completely different from the conditions familiar to us on Earth.

Many planets, by our standards, are numbingly cold or blazingly hot, so on your imaginary trip you would need the protection, and perhaps added bulk, of a climate-controlled spacesuit. On some worlds the temperature might be similar to our own, but the atmosphere might be non-existent or composed of toxic gases; you would have to carry your own air supply with you. Changes in gravity would also present you with new possibilities or challenges. On a small body, like the moon, you would be able to leap fifty feet with little effort. But if you visited a planet several times more massive than Earth, you might weigh as much as a truck, and moving about would be a very laborious process. Even if you were to go to a planet that had physical conditions almost identical to those that we take for granted here on Earth, the life forms on that planet might be totally unlike any that you have ever encountered. They could be more beautiful, more strange, more intelligent, or more ferocious than anything our own Earth has ever produced. In short, you would be exposed to conditions that lie far outside the parameters that you enjoy on your home planet.

Therefore, before venturing into any new worlds, it would be necessary to attend orientation classes that would familiarize you with the alien conditions on your destination planet. Especially since many of these conditions would prove swiftly lethal to the unprepared, you would want to understand exactly how things worked in the strange new world you were about to visit.

Now, consider for a moment that adjusting to the weird physical properties of an alien planet is small change when compared to the adjustment you had to make when you were born into this world. At the time of your birth, you moved from a non-physical realm of existence into a physical dimension of reality. Talk about encountering a new set of parameters!

At the outset, I should emphasize an important point, for it underlies everything that is to follow in this book. You and I, at the core, are spiritual beings. The physical bodies that we inhabit, and this whole physical dimension, are a small portion of the infinite, boundless Reality that is our true home. We have come to this world and put on the mantle of physicality in order to engage in certain endeavors and to learn from the results of our actions and our interactions with others.

One of the most profoundly felt and enduring dilemmas of entering into the physical world is that no orientation class instructs us about the workings of this marvelous new world. At birth, along with our physical body, we also acquire a form of amnesia, which conceals from us our larger spiritual identity and most of the knowledge and wisdom that this identity already possesses. A good portion of our work on Earth centers on remembering exactly who we really are, thus bringing the wise and radiant qualities of our spiritual identity into expression in this physical world.

The struggle to overcome our birth-induced amnesia and to couple our spiritual awareness with physical reality is arguably the most persistent and enduring endeavor of the human race. For thousands of years, human societies have chronicled their hard-won knowledge about the workings of this world, along with snatches of spiritual remembrances and insights from more subtle levels of reality. Great efforts have been made to preserve, record, and transmit this knowledge and wisdom to succeeding generations. All too frequently, however, these insights and truths become tangled up in ritual and dogma that do more to obscure than to reveal the essential teachings. It is the purpose of this book to describe and explain the fundamental qualities of our Being, and how these qualities interact with the unique conditions of this world. It is my own version of the orientation class I wish I had received when I first arrived on planet Earth.

I realize that the print medium is not interactive: an author writes the words, and a reader reads them. While I have striven to present this material in an informal and conversational tone, it is a one-way street. You may disagree and take issue with some of the points I make. As we move through this life, each one of us is influenced by any number of formal belief systems, of which there are many. Some deal with religious matters, others with politics, science, social ethics, or even art. Each belief system has a firm code of what it considers to be true and not true. One system may agree with another system on certain issues, while on other points they may differ sharply. Although it was not my intention to offend anyone, I acknowledge that many of the points I make will contradict the teachings of one belief system or another. In fact, there's probably something in this book to ruffle everyone's feathers. I encourage you to test the truth and relevance of every concept in this book. In this world, where we are all fallible, no one has a monopoly on the truth. We're going to begin with the biggest concepts first, because they underlie, inform, and influence the other topics in this book. The three fundamental qualities that govern our lives in this world, and beyond, are eternity, divinity, and unity.

Chapter One
Eternity

You are an eternal being. Every day of your life you should be aware of this reality.

What does it mean to be an eternal being? It means that you are going to live forever. Not inside the body you now inhabit, of course. Your physical body is like a vehicle you get into to go on a journey. This vehicle can take you many places, and while you are traveling within it you will see many fine sights and have many wonderful experiences. Inevitably, however, two things are going to happen: The vehicle is going to wear out and break down; and you are going to develop a yearning to see places where the vehicle cannot go. So, when the journey of an individual lifetime is complete, you leave the vehicle and embark upon your next journey.

Now, since you are encapsulated within this vehicle for the entire length of this earthly life, it is natural for you to identify with it and to believe that you and your body are one and the same. However, if you adhere to this belief, then as your body ages and its abilities decline, you will feel that your whole self is declining and deteriorating. And therefore, at the time of your death, all of your physical, mental, and spiritual attributes will have been used up and exhausted, and, as the body dies, so do you.

It is important to realize the error of rigidly identifying your Being with your body. In the same way that electricity can activate an electric motor and cause it to move about and perform tasks, your Being can animate a physical body, and cause it to walk, dance and undertake a wide range of endeavors and activities. But just as the motor is not the electric force, so too the physical body is not your being. Like energy, Being is capable of assuming many forms. Yet, in and of itself, it is eternal and indestructible.

The idea of a limitless life, of eternity that stretches on forever and forever and forever, is very difficult for the human mind to grasp, because the physical reality of our day-to-day lives involves bounded concepts. You have only so much of something, and no more. Everything has a physical limit—a quart of milk, a pound of butter. Once you use them up, they're gone; they must be replaced with new items. In our experience of this world, nothing lasts forever.

However, if you are seeking a sense of purpose and meaning for the life you are now living, it is important to see earthly life in its proper context. This life is but one chapter in a story that contains innumerable chapters—the story of your eternal existence. From our human perspective, *forever* is an incomprehensively long time, and our minds can easily become baffled by the immensity of it all.

It helps to take a leap, and to step out of the sense of chronology that you use to organize your day, your week, and your plans for the coming months. When dealing with eternity, there is no end point, no final destination, where, once you have reached it, everything stops and ends. Eternity goes on forever: *it never ends.* And neither do we. In our earthly lives, we deal with goals and destinations. From the perspective of forever, we pass through stages of development, but there are always further stages beckoning us onward. Our eternal existence is not a matter of beginnings and endings; rather, it is an ongoing process.

Think of a kaleidoscope. Each time you turn it, a beautiful image is revealed. Turn it again, and a fresh image, equally beautiful, appears. You can keep turning the kaleidoscope and enjoying one marvelous picture after another, yet at no time will you arrive at the ultimate, final image. With each turn, you merely continue a process of unfolding beauty. Our eternal existence can be viewed in a similar way; it is a continuous process of unfolding new talents, capabilities, and insights.

Your rational mind, which is accustomed to dealing in terms of limits and boundaries, is likely to have a very hard time grasping the open-ended, never-ending quality of eternity. It is likely that your mind will react with fear and resistance. So play with the idea. Daydream about your eternal nature, and explore just so many of the ramifications of forever as you are comfortable with. After all, they are not something you can lose; they'll be around forever! Just consider and investigate as much as you can without feeling threatened. If you do this, you will find yourself gradually opening up to larger and larger concepts of the richness and complexity of forever.

Once you establish comfort and confidence with the notion that you are going to go on forever, you can turn around and face in the other direction, and realize that you have already *been around* forever. Eternity extends equally as far without limit into the so-called past as it does into the future. The idea of a limitless past can be even harder to grasp than that of a limitless future.

Right now you might be asking: if I've already been around forever, and know so much, why am I stuck in this lousy job/relationship/neighborhood, etc.? I don't know the answer for you. Maybe you're a stubbornly slow learner! Kidding aside, consider that the path of your eternal lifetime has taken you through many planes of existence that are non-physical and, even when physical, non-human. So, while you're probably a master in many types of reality, the human realm is still pretty new to you.

Let's take a look at the brief period that humans have existed. Without having been present on the Earth during any particular historical epoch, the entity that is you has existed for this entire time, and it is possible that you have experienced one life or many lives in human form during this time.

Forget about whether you may have been someone famous in a previous incarnation. What is essential to realize is that, before the present bodily existence that you are now experiencing, you have lived other lives, both physical and non-physical. And in each one of these lives you have learned and developed and acquired experiences. The life that you are now living is not a continuation of all of your other lives. For example, in another lifetime you may have been a celebrated singer, while this time around you can't carry a tune in a basket. Each life has its own unique mission and purpose. There are specific lessons for you to learn in each life. Some lessons are not easy to learn, or you may be resistant to accepting them, so that you may encounter the same or similar challenges throughout several lifetimes. However, you don't enter a physical life merely to perform harsh tasks and acquire hard-won lessons, like taking a number of difficult courses in school. You also learn a great deal of value from experiences of exhilaration, wonder, and enjoyment.

As an exercise, think of all the fine homes in the area where you live. In each one of these houses, the rooms are laid out differently, the furniture and decorations are all unique, and the lives of the inhabitants are completely different from those of the residents of all the other houses. Now, imagine yourself living a rich and rewarding life in each one of those homes. You could live a complete lifetime, in each one of a hundred different houses in your local area, and in each one of those lifetimes you would encounter a range and depth of relationships and activities that would be entirely distinct from every other lifetime. All of these lives, each in its own way, would further round out an aspect of yourself. And these hundred lifetimes are easily accommodated in the smallest smidgeon of eternity.

For thousands of years almost every one of humanity's spiritual traditions and religions has taught that we are eternal beings. It is true that a number of religions have made eternal life conditional on whether or not we behave properly in our earthly life, but that is a mis-statement of the essential truth. This fallacy is very instructive, because it points up a dilemma that confronts almost everyone who enters into this physical plane. Death is a palpable and unalterable fact of physical reality. On the concrete, earthbound plane where everything can be described in hard, finite measurements, each living body reaches a transition point where the animating life separates from the visible, measured body, which then decomposes into the materials from which it was assembled. One almost overwhelming feature of physical reality is an amnesia, a forgetting, of the enduring, non-physical life we possess. So, with the exception of some psychics and mystics, each one of us, beginning in childhood, views life and existence as temporary. And we constantly see the evidence: dead plants, dead animals, dead people. We may be instructed in school or church that we possess eternal life, and we may repeat it or write it down to give a correct answer on a test. But all we are doing is saying words, and the physical evidence points quite convincingly to the opposite conclusion. So, while we have numerous spiritual teachings to show us the way, it is necessary for each one of us to come to an inner realization of our eternal nature. It is something that we know deep within ourselves, but we must awaken our present rational consciousness to this fact. This realization is not something you can acquire through someone else's say-so, it is something you must uncover and acknowledge within yourself. This process may sound overwhelmingly difficult, even impossible, to some people. Yet it is simply a matter of opening up and becoming receptive to the truth. Allow yourself to indulge in a little faith, which is the quality of accepting the reality and truth of a proposition, even when all the hard physical facts seem to point to the contrary. When you cultivate this openness, it is as if you are chiseling a little channel through all your layers of doubt. The insight will gently, and at first imperceptibly, seep through this channel into your consciousness, until, one day, BANG! You will GET IT! I don't mean to sound overly dramatic, but when you come to a full realization of one of the essential truths of your being, it is a cathartic experience.

It's more than just a mental understanding; what happens in this instance is that every cell of your being resonates with this truth. From that moment on, you own it; it is actually a part of you, and you cannot forget it or lose it. It is true that you will still be able to overlook the fact of your eternal nature and behave and act as you did before. But these will be temporary interludes, because the resonance of your realization of eternity is now vibrating within your every cell. And, over time, a thorough transformation of your attitudes will take place.

I remember vividly the moment this insight manifested, full blown, in my consciousness. I had been casually mulling the idea of eternity for several months, but not in any rigorous, organized way. It was simply a topic that would pop up now and again in odd moments of reflection.

One of my responsibilities on the estate where I live is to plow the driveway. This road is no ordinary driveway. It is more than a mile and a half in length, and it twists and climbs up and around a mountain to reach the main residence. Being in the northeastern United States, at one of the higher elevations where winter weather is typically severe, keeping this road open is frequently a challenging and dangerous task. Some years ago, we were having an especially stormy winter. The truck I was using at that time was about one wheeze away from giving up the ghost; it broke down continually. Each time I went out to plow I faced the very real prospect that the truck would expire in mid-snowstorm, and we would be snowed in with the dead hulk of the truck blocking our only avenue to the outside world. And, one day, that's exactly what happened. The truck ground to a halt in the middle of a hill and would not start. A major snowstorm was raging on top of us. Within a couple of hours, without the truck, the road would be completely impassable.

Each one of us, in our own personal terms, has a conception of utter failure, a point at which we are as good as dead. Right then, unable to fulfill my responsibility to plow the road, and with the unceasing snow making conditions worse by the minute, I had reached that point. My life was as good as over. At that moment, a strange and wondrous thing happened. A window of perception opened, and for the first time I saw clearly that the events I was experiencing could not harm or destroy me. My Being was intact and unscathed; it always had been, it always will be. In that devastating moment of failure, the calm realization of my eternal nature permeated every cell of my body. I fully understood that, through all the situations I would ever encounter—pain, pleasure, happiness, horror—I would continue to BE.

This is how the realization of my eternal nature occurred for me. The form this enlightenment takes for you will be different, yet it is as accessible to you as it was to me. All you have to do is expand your consciousness to accept it.

You may be asking why it is so important, in considering how life works on this planet, to spend so much time talking about our eternal natures, which seem to be rather removed from the nuts-and-bolts, deadline-driven demands of our physical existence. However, if you think this world and this lifetime are all there is, your thoughts and your actions will be governed by a sense of desperation. Your entire life will take on the aspect of a race you cannot win. Year after year you will be in a hurry—anxious, distrusting, and filled with a gnawing dread that everything you do is meaningless. Life will seem to be a cruel joke; this earth a torture chamber. Does this sound like the way you're living now? Or anyone you know?

At this point you may retort: So what? If I live this life like a desperate beast, at the end of it I'll find out I'm eternal, and I'll still have forever at my disposal, so who cares?

Fair question. Let's consider a life lived in desperation. Add up all the moments you have spent feeling resentment, fear, self-pity, and a host of other defeating and self-restricting emotions. Also, look at all the events and occasions when your wounded nature was too angry or fearful to extend yourself in an emotionally positive way to another person. Look at all the sadness you suffered and may have caused others. And look at all the opportunities for joy, expansion, and self-development that you have squandered. Above all, look at all the pain you have felt. So, who cares? One would think that *you* would care. You're the one who is going through all that awful pain.

Also, in this lifetime you face unique circumstances and events that will never again take place the same way. Look back on your present life to a time when a word or an act or a gesture on your part wounded someone whom you didn't mean to hurt. If you could relive that moment, behave differently, and erase that wound, wouldn't you do it? Also, look back and remember a great moment in your life: a time when you were so full of merriment that you could not stop laughing. Or the memorable look of gratitude you received from someone you had helped in a very meaningful way. Remember that touching instant when you extended solace and compassion to someone in the throes of grief. Would you go back and cancel any of those uplifting experiences? When you waste an opportunity, you remember that moment with regret, and that particular opportunity for ennobling action will not ever occur again.

Yes, we do have forever to perfect all aspects of ourselves. At the same time, on some level, everything we do, counts. Not in terms of exaltation or damnation, but in the memory of all your experiences, which resides within your soul. You know how discomforting it is to feel regret. It simply makes sense to minimize those regrettable occasions. Again, you own them; you're the one who is going to carry them and feel them.

The reason some religions posit that eternal life is conditional on your behaving the way they tell you to behave is that church leaders are human, just like you and me. The doubts and questions that you wrestle with, they wrestle with also. They have to come to the conscious realization of their eternal nature just the same as you do. And many of them, frankly, do not attain this insight.

The notion that you would only enjoy eternal life if you earned it by doing as you were told in this lifetime was concocted by religious officials who were uncertain of their own immortality. When your mind and body do not resonate with the confident realization that you are an eternal being, and you see the palpable signs of death all around you, it is easy for the mind to assemble a list of qualifications that must be met before eternal life is granted. And religious leaders labor as mightily as anyone to meet those qualifications. The major error here is thinking that eternal life begins after this earthly life ends. **You are already eternally alive.** You were alive before you were born into this world, and the moment of your death is nothing more than a doorway through which you pass from one dimension of reality into another. You don't have to qualify for an everlasting life; it is something that is already yours, irrevocably. Good works and a virtuous life are worthwhile on their own terms, but they neither permit nor deny you life after death.

Consider that both the scope of reality and the depth of your being are so vast that the physical human brain simply cannot comprehend it all. In order for you to function in the material plane, the extent of your awareness must be narrowed down to a very tiny focus. That focus illuminates the physical surroundings and workings of this world. When you are born, you forget about the multiple other levels of your being so that you can concentrate on the tasks you came here to perform.

When you do recover a thoroughgoing awareness of your eternal nature, a marvelous transformation can then occur in the way you live your life. When you are living a life of desperation, you feel threatened on all sides. You are always only one step away from disaster. The thinking that dominates your mind runs something like this: "If I don't get this promotion; if I don't close this deal; win this contract; get so-and-so to go out with me on Saturday night..., it's all over for me. My life will be ruined. I'll never feel like showing my face in public. I'll never smile again."

When you live life in this manner, the prevailing image is that of walking on a tightrope. If every single thing does not go right, if you take just one misstep, you will plummet into the black depths of the abyss, never to be heard from again. See how this thinking has plotted out your entire life in a linear fashion, where each event in your life is crucially linked to the ones before and after it? There is no room for error, and annihilation dogs your every step.

Once you remember and fully acknowledge that you are eternal, you gain the confidence that, whatever may happen, you will come through it and exist on the other side. If certain plans don't work out, your circumstances may be more difficult for a while, but you will still be around. And you will smile again. Even the ultimate mishap of this world, death, will no longer be seen as an ending, but only a transition. In the light of this understanding, a new picture will emerge. Instead of being a person on a tightrope, you are a cork, floating on the ocean. There may be occasional storms with deep swells, and towering waves may crash over your head, but you will always, always, come bobbing back up to the surface. You may get tossed about, but you cannot sink. The entire ocean, which is the universe, *is holding you up!* Being eternal means that you are indestructible and inextinguishable. Whatever happens to you, no matter how frightening or awful, you will survive it. You may change form, but you will persist, and you will go on. So enjoy your life. You're going to be living it for a long, long, long, long time.

Even after you have attained a visceral realization of your eternal nature, it will still be possible, even likely, for you to get caught up in temporal affairs and slip back into thinking and acting out of desperation. What you need to do is remind yourself, frequently, that you are eternal. Unfortunately, the workings of most societies are organized in such a way that they perpetuate the false notion that this world is all there is, and so the parameters of the workplace, school, and social life all reinforce the mentality of desperation. Learn to go against the grain. The more you contemplate eternity, the more familiar it will become for you. And as you look into it, you will find your concepts of life and being constantly broadening.

To be aware of your eternal nature is a fundamental key to understanding how life works in this world and your purpose in being here. We will frequently refer back to this essential truth as we consider other elements and aspects of existence and how they fit into the expression and conduct of life here on Earth.

Chapter Two
Divinity

Throughout the ages and all around the world, people have felt that there is something greater than themselves. This conviction goes much deeper than respect and awe for the natural forces of wind and rain, volcano and earthquake, that make us seem so puny and powerless. We sense that there is an Intelligence, a comprehensively aware Being, which is the true source of our life and our consciousness. At the very deepest levels of our own awareness, there is a recognition, profoundly felt yet inexpressible, that we are linked to this Source Being. Many terms and names have been formulated to refer to this Being: God, Allah, Yahweh, the Creator, Manitou, the Great Spirit, Divine Oneness.

My own term of preference is the All-There-Is. I like this term because it is open ended and boundless. As I grow and gain more insight, my conception of the universe and existence keeps getting bigger and more multi-layered. If I had a static, rigidly defined picture of a Divine Being, it would lose its relevance as my knowledge of the universe expanded. But the All-There-Is, by definition, contains *All-There-Is,* that which I now know, as well as everything that is presently unknown to me, but is still a part of existence.

Not too many years ago, astronomers estimated that there were no more than ten billion galaxies in the universe. Then the Hubble Space Telescope was launched, and we were able to observe more distant regions of space. In light of our expanded observational capabilities, it is now estimated that there are at least fifty billion galaxies in the universe. And there may be more, many more, that are beyond the limit of what we can presently observe.

Also, until very recently, mainstream science held that our three-dimensional universe was the sum total of existence. But now physicists and cosmologists openly discuss multiple dimensions of reality, and multi-verses of existence, which may be as numerous as all the stars in all the galaxies—essentially limitless.

Consider that the entire vast universe we know about—as well as all the other possible dimensions that we can only, at present, speculate about—are all contained within the consciousness of the All-There-Is. I know this is asking a lot, because as human beings we operate within a very tiny frame of reference. So let's come back to our own Earth, this little stony satellite of the Sun. When we allow our consciousness to freely contemplate both the immensity and the inclusiveness of the All-There-Is, we will begin to realize that this Supreme Being created all we see around us—clouds, mountains, forests, seas—and is All.

From this realization we can view all of creation as divine, precious, and holy. There is no garbage, refuse, or junk in creation. Every particle is inalienably imbued with the vibration of the Divine. So, you are God. As is every other person, and thing, that you encounter. We are all a portion of the All-There-Is.

Not only are you an eternal being, you are divine in nature. As with your eternal soul, the spark of divinity you embody is inextinguishable and inseparable from you. On Earth we make a widespread practice of casting out and ostracizing all sorts of criminals, reprobates, miscreants and others that civilized society deems to be insufferable. The worst of the lot are locked away in prisons, the rest are, in one or several ways, avoided or shunned. And beyond this earthly existence, we have devised the concepts of excommunication and damnation to permanently shut out those sinners, transgressors, and tyrants who have committed acts that we deem unforgivable.

This outlook may be a convenient and useful mental construct, but in the scheme of the much larger reality, it just isn't so. Every entity, no matter how abhorrently they behave, still carries a divine spark. By definition, nothing can stand outside of All-There-Is. Everything and everyone is included, forever.

Let's say you go to the theater to see a play. One of the characters is a thoroughgoing villain. He lies and steals and murders, and over the course of the story almost every character is reduced to misery and poverty because of his misdeeds. In the final scene he is defeated by the hero, and you cheer lustily when the fatal blow is struck and this horrible person collapses in a lifeless heap.

When the play is over, you linger outside the theater, chatting with some friends. After a while the actors, having removed their costumes and makeup, emerge from the stage door. In street clothes they appear different from the way they looked onstage, but you recognize the actor who played the hero, the leading lady, the widow, and—there he is—the villain. Only he's not a villain, he's an actor, laughing and joking with the other members of the cast. The part of the villain was a role that he enacted upon the stage. When he steps off the stage, he sheds that repulsive persona along with his fake mustache and period costume.

Keep in mind that we are all divine entities who put on the costume of a physical body in order to act upon the stage of this Earth. Not all of our actions are perfect. In fact, if they were, there would be no point in coming here in the first place. It is through imperfect actions—making mistakes—that we learn, and thus grow in knowledge and wisdom. And some of our actions will be more imperfect, hurtful, and destructive than others. Some will be downright cruel and criminal. However, we need to be able to separate the entity from the action. Outside of this world, each person's actions—even depraved actions—can be seen in a neutral light, as lessons for that entity, and others. The actions of a murderous tyrant can be instructive to all the members of the society which that tyrant misruled, as well as to outside observers and succeeding generations. The entity who embodied those actions probably had huge lessons to learn from them, but also served, like the actor playing a villain, as a focal point to draw attention to specific ways of behaving and relating to others.

Beyond our earthbound and humanly defined concepts of right and wrong, good and bad, honorable and damnable, there is the vastly larger reality in which everything is, and remains, divine. To fully live in this world, and to begin to understand the place of earthly experience within the context of larger layers of reality, we must open ourselves to the point of being able to acknowledge the divinity in everyone we meet, and in every plant, every animal, each stone, raindrop, and speck of dust. Everything is divine; everything is sacred.

This concept runs completely counter to our prevalent mode of thinking in which we are constantly dividing the world into opposing camps of friends and enemies, good and bad, that which we love and that which we hate. We need to develop the ability to step outside of these rigid, linear constructs. This practice of the rational mind is useful in comparing and evaluating relative degrees of desirability with respect to our personal preferences. But just because you like apples and you don't like oranges, it doesn't mean that there is anything bad about oranges. Everything that is in this universe belongs in this universe. It is an inalienable part of creation, and has the same claim to being a portion of the Divine as we have.

The challenge for us, in every moment, is to recognize and honor the Divine identity in everything we encounter. Sounds like a tall order, doesn't it? Can you presently salute the divinity of the flies buzzing over the fruit in your kitchen, the neighbor's dog who just dug up your flower bed, or the moron in the car ahead of you, who's moping along at ten miles under the speed limit, while you're late for an appointment? No wonder we're eternal. It's probably going to take that long before we can embrace all of those irritating entities!

But that's all part of our journey of learning. Years ago it occurred to me that the fundamental task of a human life is to refine ourselves to the point where we are able to respond lovingly to every person, situation, and thing. The very idea of responding lovingly to every annoying, hurtful, and frustrating person and event in our lives may at first appear impossible, blocked by insurmountable barriers. But that is only because, since early childhood, we have been conditioned to complain, form oppositions, and assign blame to anything that discomfits or inconveniences us in any way. This habit of demeaning and ostracizing anyone or anything that displeases us is a process of denying the divinity of other persons and things. And it is an illusion, the fabrication of a shortsighted mentality that feels hurt and offended. Once we understand this illusion for what it is, and step out of the petty practice of regarding others as flawed, unfit, and unworthy, we will be able to perceive more of their radiant, heavenly natures.

For most of us, this transformation will not take place overnight. For many years we have been trained to criticize and devalue others, and a significant portion of society perpetuates these attitudes and projects them at us every day. Step by step, one experience at a time, we need to enlarge our awareness of the sacred nature of everything. As we do so, our cranky, divinity-denying attitudes will lose their relevance and appeal, and slip away.

Here is a saying I have encountered several times in various spiritual teachings: "The god in me salutes the god in you." Allow your consciousness to expand into the larger framework of seeing everything as a holy, eternally included part of the All-There-Is. A marvelous thing will happen. The more frequently you recognize and salute the divinity in others, the more often you will see it in yourself. As you increasingly perceive the divinity all around you, you will become less judgmental and more accepting. You will find yourself growing into a greater appreciation of every element in the world around you.

It will always be challenging to acknowledge the divine element within each obnoxious and unpleasant entity we encounter each day. And, beyond that, we must confront our feelings and reactions to the violent and malicious acts of people who have become so twisted by their own pain and hatred that they seem to be beyond rehabilitation and redemption, and thus undeserving of our consideration. However, it is precisely in these instances where we have the greatest opportunity to grow in understanding and to expand our capacity to accept, forgive, and, yes, even to love. The most violent and depraved of individuals, though he may not show it, has a heart, needs food, is susceptible to disease, and will die just like everyone else. If anything, such a person probably experiences more inner turmoil and pain than most people. His present life is likely a tortured one, in which he is confronted with big lessons to learn. He has laughed and cried, felt compassion and fear, just as we have. His acts may be more reprehensible than anything you have ever done, but he will move on from this life and go on for eternity, learning and growing, just as everyone else will. He may be so prone to violence and destruction that he is a consistent threat to public safety and well-being, and incarceration may be the only way to curb his violent tendencies. Keep in mind that, at a deeper level, the actor is separate from his actions, and that under everyone's costume, hero and villain alike, is a Divine being.

There is another aspect of divinity that we should explore here, and that is the personal relationship each one of us has with the All-There-Is. We all have our own conception of God. Many times it is the picture that was presented to us by whatever religious training we may have had. Common conceptions of God picture a Being that is loving, kind, knowing, powerful, and above all, personal, in that God knows who we are, what we want, what we've done, etc. Also, God is responsive to our entreaties. We may not always receive exactly what we pray for, but we are assured that our prayers are received by a knowing, receptive Being, who can effect direct and specific actions on our behalf.

Regardless of our religious background, and even if we have had none, the tendency to appeal to a higher power in times of danger or acute need pervades all cultures and classes. Even agnostics and atheists, faced with severe peril, will plead for assistance from a force that, in their safer moments, they take great pride in denying.

This activity usually proceeds unconsciously. Most people would probably say that they don't formally pray for success in mundane matters. Yet each one of us in our heart silently sends out entreaties for favorable outcomes many times each day. They aren't addressed to anyone in particular, and we wouldn't call them prayers. But we send forth a constant stream of requests: that the store hasn't closed; that the boss approves of our work; that the person who ignites a flame of attraction in our breast responds to us with acceptance and affection. We believe that we are a good and deserving person, and that there is some larger consciousness which knows it too, and regards us with at least passive favor.

At a level of awareness that is deeper than our waking consciousness and rarely conceptualized with words, we maintain the memory of having grown out of the All-There-Is. Since we are inextricably and unseverably connected with this Source Being, communicating our needs and requests to it is the most natural thing we can do.

Some of us may have a hard time admitting that any One Being could possibly know us, and every other person, plant, animal, and speck of matter on a personal level. For some it may seem to be a numerically impossible task, for others it may sound like a naïve fairy tale. After all, we are capable of independent actions, and many of us do truly deplorable things. How can any Being, no matter how knowledgeable or powerful, possibly be aware of everything that is happening at all times and have the capacity for direct involvement in any and every event?

What is lacking in this question is not the ability of the All-There-Is, but rather the small scope of our own comprehension and imagination. We humans think we're pretty smart. After all, we've shaped much of this planet's surface to suit our own purposes. We've split the atom and put men on the moon. However, moment to moment, as you go through your day, how cognizant are you of what's going on in your own body? When you take a breath, do you consciously instruct the blood cells in your lungs to release carbon dioxide and other waste products, and then to latch onto oxygen? Do you tell your heart when and how vigorously to beat, or consciously direct the digestion of the food you eat? Your body contains trillions of cells, and every second, in every one of those cells, millions of separate chemical reactions are occurring, all for the single purpose of sustaining and extending your life. It is your lifeforce that animates your body and directs your autonomic nervous system.

On the level of your waking consciousness, how much do *you* really know or understand about your body? You didn't design it, and many times you have a hard time getting it to do precisely what you want it to do, like shedding those ten (or more) pounds of excess weight. And while you may, for the most part (weight loss aside), believe that you are the master of your body, you are no match for your autonomic nervous system. This is the system that controls most of your body's functions, such as respiration, circulation, and digestion, without any conscious input from you. In fact, the autonomic nervous system can override your conscious commands. For example, if you decided to hold your breath until you died, the autonomic nervous system would first withhold oxygen from your brain, so that you would lose consciousness and pass out. Once you were unconsciousness, it would resume the breathing process, and your life would go on.

Stretch your imagination for a moment, and picture a Being capable of designing every organ, tissue, and cell in your body, down to the last atom. Bear in mind that this Being *lives within* every molecule and subatomic particle in existence, so that it can experience each atomic interaction as vividly as you experience a toothache, or the embrace of a loved one. It is aware of every chemical reaction taking place in every cell, as well as the actions, thoughts, and emotions of the organism as a whole. Such a level of knowledge and awareness is far beyond human comprehension. But for the All-There-Is, such awareness is a root ability. Just as our autonomic nervous system possesses a much more extensive awareness of all the activities occurring in our bodies than our mind can comprehend, so too the awareness of the All-There-Is intimately perceives *all-there-is.*

Within such an all-pervading and all-encompassing Consciousness, our personal concerns and aspirations are well known, and receive appropriate consideration. To be sure, not all of our wishes will be granted. It's not that we're being punished. Rather, life in this dimension involves give and take, both setbacks and triumphs. Often, we learn greater lessons and are spurred on to more improvement through our defeats than through our victories.

We will all encounter periods when we are beset with failure and rejection. At such times we may feel alone and forsaken; we may despair that there is anything beyond the awful pain we are enduring. The world seems to be an insensible and impersonal collection of molecules randomly colliding. Life is senseless and there is nothing beyond it. There is no God, and there is no love. At times such as these, what we are doing is attempting to separate ourselves from the rest of existence and being, withdrawing into a cocoon of self-pity. In effect, we are excommunicating ourselves from the universe and exiling ourselves into a self-made hell.

Understand that neither this world nor the All-There-Is ever expels or excommunicates us. The movement toward exile and alienation comes from within us, and it stems from our hurt feelings because we have been disappointed or thwarted. At such times the thing to keep remembering is that we are not forsaken. Beneath our temporary pain and suffering we remain connected to the All-There-Is, and the inextinguishable spark of our divinity steadily burns. The more we keep in mind our intrinsic holiness, the easier it will be to step out of our shell of isolation and re-engage with those around us.

Each one of us is an essential and valuable component of this universe. When we become muddied and bloodied with the affairs of this world we may not feel so godly. But, through it all, we are all recognized and beloved portions of the All-There-Is.

Chapter Three
Unity

The third member of our trinity of big concepts is unity. All is One. This idea may be the hardest one to accept and understand. It's comforting to know that you will exist forever. It's also uplifting to realize that, despite your failings and sometimes reproachable behavior, you will never be beyond redemption, for you are a particle of the Divine. On its face, unity seems to assault our cherished notion of independent individuality, and the ego resists this idea, for it seems to threaten its very nature. Besides, our rational experience in this three-dimensional world tells us that things are very distinct and separate.

However, what is most grating about the idea of unity is the thought that we have a common identity with every person we encounter on Earth. Imagine a person with whom you have argued, even fought. Terrible things were said by you and to you; your heart harbors an undying enmity for this person. You never want to see or speak to them again. Ever. At one time you may have been friends or co-workers, but there has been a complete rupture in your relationship; from this point, your paths diverge. You will go your separate ways, moving ever farther apart, forever. I'm sure everyone has experienced such a break and knows the feeling of wanting to exile the offending party to the outer reaches of the universe. Because of the way we have been hurt, cheated or insulted, we want to negate and alienate the other person. It's a tremendous challenge to acknowledge that this person continues to carry a Divine spark, just like ourselves and everyone else. What is a hundred times more difficult is to even entertain the notion that you and this awful person are ultimately joined, and share in the one, unified identity of All-There-Is.

Don't become too concerned about being forced into any distasteful reconciliations. Your conscious focus in this world is an exceedingly narrow one. When you die, the ego personality that suffered and held onto the memories of every slight and insult will dissolve like frost on a warm spring morning. The positions that you took and adhered to so firmly in this lifetime will be seen as a superficial film that filtered your experiences, and you will discard them. The whole dualistic framework of oppositions, which is a defining feature of this world, will dissolve. The same process will happen for your supposed enemy. As you both shed your conflicting ideas, positions, and actions, which surrounded you like two clashing costumes of clothes, you will again recognize each other as kindred souls. This doesn't mean that you will merge together and lose your own identities, only that the mark of your common ultimate identity will be more apparent.

And, even in this lifetime, separations that both parties regarded as permanent and everlasting have, over time, transformed into reconciliations. It has frequently happened that two people who marry each other in youth are ill-equipped to resolve their inevitable differences of opinion and competing priorities. The stresses of the modern economy add strain to the relationship. They spend long hours involved with their jobs, and they never seem to have adequate time to communicate with each other their views and desires. Trivial issues are not resolved, and become the building blocks for bigger disagreements. The couple begins to argue and resent each other deeply. Finally they divorce, disgusted with the sight of each other, saying, "This in not the person I married." When they part, they feel they are well rid of each other.

Then a funny thing happens. Years pass. Both of them grow and mature. One day they may bump into each other, strike up a conversation, and find that they enjoy each other's company. In some instances, the flame of attraction may be rekindled. They may date, fall in love all over again, and remarry. More often, they will simply reestablish a relationship as friends. In these instances, the friendship is renewed, not because one party has come to their senses and mended their ways, but because both parties have matured and changed. Even in this world, there is always the possibility of resolution and reconciliation. In the larger, eternal reality, all the issues that divide us here are like the differing colors of team uniforms. They cease to matter when we leave the playing field.

Still, you're probably asking how can so many diverse elements, forces, ideas, and things all belong to one common whole? The following metaphors may not be entirely adequate, but they will serve as a starting point. Look at the hairs on your forearm. They may be thick or thin, and you probably haven't noticed them in some while, but they're there. Take a moment and become cognizant of the surprising multitude that are there. Each one is separate and distinct. They may curve or bend in a variety of directions. Picture each one as a person, walking down a wide street, purchasing groceries in a marketplace. After all, each one is an individual. Now, widen your focus of attention, and notice the obvious: they are all growing out of your arm. One arm; hundreds of individual hairs. To take this analogy a step further, consider the hairs on a calico cat. The animal is covered with many thousands of individual hairs, and they come in several colors. Most are very fine and of moderate length. Yet some, like the whiskers, are quite long and much thicker. An uncountable number of hairs, of varying lengths, colors, and qualities. All growing out of one cat.

To expand this concept yet further, look at the Earth. Spinning along in space, it is a solitary unit. Living on and in this planet are millions of different species of life: microorganisms, plants, and animals. The number of living individuals of all species runs up beyond the trillions, yet all of them have grown out of the material of the Earth, and all share the single identity of being Earthlings. There are all kinds of conflicting actions and processes occurring every moment, yet the whole Earth is one system, one unit.

If this example is too much of a stretch, consider your own body. It is composed of trillions of cells, each one of which functions not only harmoniously with the whole organism but also autonomously by taking in nutrients and excreting wastes, and generally pursuing its own self-sustaining course. And within your body, some cells attack or dismantle other cells. There is cooperation, competition, and conflict, all within a single body. How do you regard your body? As an amalgamation of departments—tissues, organs, blood, bones, nails, nerves, and teeth? Or do you see it as a whole, a unit?

In a very real sense, in our relationship to the immensity of the All, we are much the same as a single cell in relationship to our body. Each cell is an integral, essential part of the total organism, yet at the same time it pursues an autonomous, self-sustaining course, sometimes competing with other cells for supplies and nutrients. Within unity, cooperation and conflict do not merely coexist side by side, they blend and meld together like the multiple currents of water in a rocky stream, which continually weave together and split apart. Sometimes flowing together and sometimes taking separate paths, they are all composed of the same substance, water.

Unity can accommodate a vast, vast spectrum of differentiation and individuation. Once we get past our fear that, by accepting Unity, our identity might somehow get gobbled up and go out of existence, we can delve a little bit into the mystery that we are a portion of the All. It will then become easier—in fact inviting—to penetrate below the level of our conscious ego, in which we have invested so much of our sense of personal identity. Below this level we are still a distinct consciousness, yet here we can perceive more of the underlying kinship that we share with other persons, as well as with other forms of life. And even with so-called inanimate matter.

Our scientific understanding of the properties of chemical compounds and various physical forces has been advanced by many persons who have been able to go beneath the surface of the isolated, distinct object they were studying and achieve a sort of common viewpoint—to feel what it feels, want what it wants. Indeed, at the very tiniest levels of physical investigations, it has been discovered and acknowledged that the beliefs and feelings of experimenters directly influence the behavior of the particles they are studying. It's as if these very tiny particles, which are many times smaller than a single atom, align and merge their identity with that of the experimenter.

In our daily lives we experience moments of unity with other individuals and groups of persons. Frequently, in conversation with another person, we will enter into a state of agreement where we both share the same idea and goal. And, beyond mental agreement, there are those moments when, through the exchange of meaningful eye-to-eye contact, we *know* that our feelings and understanding are at one with another person.

Then there are those occasions when groups of people, from small gatherings to multitudes of thousands, will merge themselves into a single identity. Think of sporting events. Whether it's a highschool basketball game or a professional contest in a huge stadium, the supporters of a team will put aside all of their social, ethnic, and religious differences to cheer and chant together, effectively becoming one identity. In the same way, the audience at a play or concert will be collectively captivated by a brilliant performance, and at the end of the show they will all join in a common outpouring of appreciation and applause.

There are still larger examples of this phenomenon. Such as war. At such times, an entire country will be caught up in the fervor to march off and fight with some other nation. Even though a minority of the population may dissent, the prevailing policy will redirect the purpose of the national economy from production to destruction. Each citizen will be as one cell in the national organism, which is fighting to survive against a foreign attacker. There will be huge rallies in support of the troops and their cause, and the mass consciousness of the nation will be focused upon the affairs of war until the conflict has ended.

If you reflect on it a bit, you will discover that we merge our identities with others numerous times each day. From children reciting the alphabet in unison, to a group of friends laughing at a joke, to that scintillating moment when you and another person are on exactly the same wavelength, our distinct identities enter into juncture points where we meld with other identities, while still retaining our individuality. Like individual grain stalks on a vast prairie, each one of us is rooted into the overarching consciousness of the All-There-Is, of which we are an inseparable, divine, and eternal part.

Chapter Four
Duality

Eternity, divinity, and unity are inherent qualities of our souls, our inner beings. We possess these qualities whether we are in a physical body or not, whether we are in this dimension, this universe, or someplace else. There is another quality that, as far as I can tell, is much more specific to human consciousness on Earth. It is a quality of the way we think. Since most or all of the other life forms on this planet do not possess the same mental framework and viewpoint that we do, this quality may be uniquely human. It serves as a lens through which we see and react to this world; thus it is extremely influential in how we live. It is so pervasive that it is taken for granted and rarely thought about, yet it is to our advantage to understand this quality: what it is and how it operates.

The quality I am referring to is *duality*, which is the mental process of splitting the world and our experience into opposing segments. Some examples are: hot-cold, light-dark, happy-sad, beautiful-ugly, good-evil. It may be that the act of developing a rational, word based-mentality contains within it a tendency toward regarding the world in dualistic terms.

Keep in mind that this world is a unit, a whole. In the terms of this physical world, existence is in three dimensions. Imagine a sphere. It has height, width, and depth. Our emotions also possess three-dimensional characteristics, in that our feelings are all encompassing. They have a depth to them. In contrast, our rational thinking is a linear, one-dimensional process. We string words along in a line, one word after another.

The rational mind cannot apprehend three dimensions simultaneously. In one instant, it apprehends height and width. Then, the next instant, it switches to comprehend depth.

When we think, we have to proceed all the way to the end of the sentence to find out whether "The apple is ..." yellow or red. When we gaze at an apple, no words are necessary, for the sense impression of the apple's color is instantaneous. Likewise, when we feel an emotion, we don't think our way into it. The emotion wells up, full blown and unmistakable, all at once. With words alone we can never adequately describe love, but we can feel it.

Still, it is with our minds and our thinking that we appraise the workings of the world, make our plans, and assess the results of our actions. We need our thinking faculty, but we use it so much that we don't realize that it's only giving us a partial picture of the world.

Before you entered this world, you were not a thinking being. When you were a young child, you were actually taught how to think, to describe objects and formulate concepts in words. Observe a baby or young toddler. They have a conscious awareness of themselves and their surroundings, and it is very obvious that they feel things fully and can express the full spectrum of emotions from joy and delight to fear, loneliness, and anger. However, at this point they are not thinking. They have yet to acquire the whole rational construct of apprehending and describing objects, their experiences, and their feelings in word-based, linear terms. Since they are surrounded by a family and society that constantly employs this rational framework, children will soon learn words. A little later, due to the unrelenting influence of parents and other well wishers, the children will string words together into intelligible sentences. In this way they will acquire language and all the rational rules and assumptions that embody it.

You have been thinking, almost non-stop, for many years now. You are so accustomed to thinking that it would be hard, if not impossible, for you to go back to the time in your life before you acquired language and thought, and to recall what your earliest awareness and perceptions were like. To illustrate just how exclusively you now use your thinking faculty, try this exercise: Sit quietly for a couple of minutes and empty your mind of all thoughts. See if you can make it a blank slate, free of all thought, even stray words. You will find that the rational faculty will seize upon the slightest hint of a stimulus to resume thinking full tilt.

All this thinking can serve many constructive purposes. Indeed, you would not be where you are in your life today if you hadn't first formed the picture and then materialized it with your thoughts. But rational thinking has its limitations. Because we think in linear terms, with our minds alone, we never get a fully formed, three-dimensional picture of what we are thinking about. Also, one of the root activities of thinking is to compare and evaluate. We consider one thing in comparison, or contrast, to something else. An object weighs more or less, is taller or shorter, softer or harder, than another object. We do this all the time, separating and splitting one thing away from everything else so that we can describe it in terms that will allow everyone else who uses our language to know exactly what we are talking about when we say certain words and phrases. Along with delineating the objects of this world according to their physical properties, we also describe them in comparative qualitative terms, such as hot or cold, useful or useless, beautiful or ugly, appetizing or nauseating. If we're not careful, we can extend this rational tendency to the point where we regard some things (and people) as good, and others as bad.

Remember, however, that all is one. We are all members of one unified system. In physical reality it is indeed useful to be able to distinguish and choose those things and courses of action that will best ensure our survival, prosperity, and happiness. But we must remain ever mindful that everything, and everyone, belongs here, whether we find them suitable to our own preferences or not. Be aware that the rational faculty, which you use all the time, habitually splits and segregates whatever it is thinking about into opposing categories. Since our thinking never gives us the full, three-dimensional picture, the oppositions that the mind formulates will also be lacking the dimension of depth. Thus, the opposition will never be as neat or strictly defined as the rational report makes it out to be.

Traditional and aboriginal societies from around the globe have cautioned against regarding anything in absolute terms as belonging exclusively to one extreme or the other. Native Americans have long maintained that no person or thing is so bad that it does not contain a grain of good in it. And that even the most beautiful or delightful thing will invariably contain a flaw. They understood that everything is a portion of the overarching unity of All. And while something may exhibit properties or aspects that we consider destructive or distasteful, it is only that we are viewing it from a single perspective, and from that angle its pleasing and constructive attributes are not visible. Still, they are there, because the object is whole. What is incomplete is our vision. Especially as it is seen through the linear rational faculty.

A number of societies, particularly those in the Pacific Islands, have avoided the fallacy of splitting the world into good and bad, or good and evil. For them, there is good, and not-good. That which is not-good may be unappealing, untimely, or inappropriate. But it is not bad. It is simply not preferred, as that which is regarded as good will be chosen instead of it.

For example, I *love* chocolate. For me, chocolate isn't merely good, it's great, wonderful, the most satisfying taste in the world. A piece of chocolate layer cake is my dessert of choice after a fine dinner. However, if I were offered a second piece of cake after I finished the first, it would not be good. There's nothing wrong with the second piece of cake; it's exactly the same as the first. But at this point I have eaten my fill, and any additional food, even luscious chocolate, would only give me indigestion.

We have an age-old expression, "too much of a good thing." It aptly describes the pivotal point at which something goes from being good to not-good. The thing itself has not changed. In my example above, the inherent properties of chocolate are a forever valued part of this world, where everything is an outgrowth of the Divine. My own desire or aversion for chocolate depends upon my changing tastes and appetites.

In modern society, the tendency to split the world into good and bad leads to a great deal of irritation and trouble. If you allow your mind to consistently set up oppositions where it accepts what it considers as good and consequently rejects whatever is on the other side of the equation, which you have qualitatively defined as bad, you will wind up rejecting at least half the world. As a good illustration, examine your own present dislikes and prejudices. We tend to like and feel comfortable with people who look, sound, behave, and dress the same as we do. To a greater or lesser degree, we feel discomfort around people who, by the color of their skin or style of dress, look different from us. If they sound different and speak another language, there is an additional element of threat because we can't understand everything they're saying. Our level of unease and distrust rises further if these people have different religious beliefs, cultural practices, and political systems than we have. So, even though we are all members of a single human race, we find ourselves belittling, rejecting , and demonizing people that our dualistic thinking has defined as being opposed to ourselves. And the list of potential oppositions we can construct is virtually endless: black-white, Christian-Moslem, communist-capitalist, meat eater-vegetarian, Republican-Democrat, sports fan-theatergoer, creationist-evolutionist, and on and on and on.

It is said that politics makes for strange bedfellows, because people who are vehemently opposed to each other on one or several issues will often join forces in support of a particular candidate or issue. Given our tendency to divide and oppose, any pairing of human beings can be considered a strange coupling; each one of us can find one or more issues on which we will differ with everyone else in the world. Each time we form a sentence, we have the potential to set up yet another division between ourselves and others.

One very curious feature of the tendency toward dualism is that often it only takes the slightest bit of influence one way or the other to turn us into a staunch advocate or fierce opponent of a particular idea or issue. With a little self examination we will all probably remember a time when we strongly supported an idea that we now oppose, or vice versa. As an illustration of how easy it is to become engrossed in a dualistic opposition, watch a contest in a sport that doesn't interest you, involving two teams that you know nothing about. Choose a team to root for in an arbitrary way, by flipping a coin. Then observe how strongly your emotions are engaged by the fluctuating fortunes of this team as the game unfolds. Even though the outcome of this contest will have no impact on your personal affairs—and you don't even care for the sport—you will feel elated if your team wins, and, at the very least, disappointed if they lose.

Opposing forces, in and of themselves, are neither good nor bad. They are simply half circles, which, when combined, restore that relationship to unity. Take weather, for example. In a high-pressure system, the air circulates clockwise and the weather is generally sunny. A low-pressure system has a counter clockwise circulation and generates rain and storms. For life as we know it to persist on this planet, we need a combination of sun and showers. If it never rained, the earth would be all desert. If it rained all the time, most plants would perish from lack of sunlight and nutrient depletion of the soil.

Keep in mind that, over the course of your life, you are going to take sides on any number of issues and engage in various movements, campaigns, and struggles. You are in this world to strive, to exercise your muscles and your mind. But it is also good to remember that the whole playing field on Earth is just that—a playing field; a stage on which to assume a part and act.

The etymology of the word *part* can be very enlightening. First, a *part,* or *particle,* is a portion or segment of a whole. By its very nature, it is incomplete. In politics, adherents of certain philosophies and policies assemble themselves into *parties,* and if you are especially vigorous in promoting one point of view versus all others, you will be referred to as a *partisan.* When we closely define an item according to its unique attributes and qualities, we are being *particular.* And when we take sides in an issue and devote our energies and efforts to seeing that this issue is resolved in favor of the side we support, be it a political debate, a business enterprise, or a sporting contest, we are *participating.*

In all of these cases, we are aligning ourselves and our actions with one portion of a larger whole. The unstated understanding behind the use of the word *part-* is that there is a greater and all-encompassing whole.

A number of the world's great creation myths speak of the splitting of the fundamental unity into darkness and light, land and sea, earth and sky, and a host of other polar opposites. *Polar* is indeed an apt word. Envision a pole, which is a line with two ends. On one end we place a quality such as light, and on the other end, its opposite, dark. The dualistic division of the world into opposing qualities can be represented in this linear fashion, with each quality at one end, or pole, of the line. Remember that thinking is a linear process; we string words into thoughts one after another. Our tendency to split the world into dualistic oppositions stems directly from this fundamental property of thought. Whoever formulated these creation myths understood the unity of All and how the physical world is an arena encompassed by unity. They used the literary convention of contending gods and forces to erect an understandable framework of how we use our rational faculty to create a dualistic world of oppositions in which we can strive, pursue our lessons, and act out our dramas.

In the biblical story of Creation, Adam and Eve lived in union with God, and Eden was Paradise. However, within this garden was the Tree of Knowledge of good and evil. What is the knowledge of good and evil? It is the ability to split the unity of existence into opposing, dualistic qualities. That is, the ability to think. What happens when Adam and Eve eat the fruit of this Tree of Knowledge? They begin to think linearly, and thus fracture the world into sets of dualistic oppositions. From that moment on, they begin to regard everything in terms of desirable and undesirable, tasty and nauseating, treasure and garbage.

By thinking in terms of opposition, separating the world into that which we love and that which we hate, we exile ourselves from Paradise. When we place ourselves into the state of mentally regarding the world in dualistic terms, we can expect to know pleasure and pain, play and toil; there will be moments of lightness and fun, as well as times of darkness and despair. Spiritual and religious traditions down through the ages have maintained that heaven is a state of union with God, while hell is a state of separation and alienation.

The key point to understand is that our indestructible essence is forever in union with the All-There-Is. It is only with our linear, dualistic thoughts that we create the illusion of exiling ourselves from the rest of creation. Even though it is a self-generated illusion, however, our rational, one-dimensional minds believe it. The resulting sense of being forsaken, and the anguish we feel, is palpable and real.

Each day there is the likelihood that your thoughts will form oppositions that will engender varying degrees of alienation from friends, family, and associates. To counteract this tendency, develop the habit of reminding yourself numerous times each day that unity is the underlying state of the universe. Everything is connected. And each person and thing, with all of its individual properties and traits, grows directly out of the One. We all have a common origin and, ultimately, a common identity. Duality is a subset of unity. All opposing qualities are encompassed within the whole. For example, consider this planet. There are hot places and cold regions. There are watery seas and dry land. Fertile places and deserts. You could compile a long list of all the opposite features one could find here. Yet, seen from space, it is one planet. All of these seeming contradictions are accommodated within this single sphere. In the same way, unity encompasses duality, joining all together.

I believe it is helpful for each one of us to be mindful that this is the way that our reality is constructed. As humans, we are thinking beings, and each day our thoughts form hundreds, if not thousands, of opposing situations. Many of them are pretty simple and harmless, such as, "do I want apple juice or orange juice with breakfast?" But the tendency of our linear thinking is to place things (and people) at opposite ends of a line, and to imply a tension, or opposition between the two ends.

In the great majority of our thoughts, we place ourselves at one end of our linear thought line. Then, elements of our world, and other people, are placed at the other pole. In this way, the tendency is to see each one of our relationships in terms of an opposition. Sometimes, the content of the thought is to draw the two ends of the line together, as in, "Mary is my friend." Frequently, though, the thought will describe and reinforce a difference or division between ourselves and another. Such as, "Dave is not as good a swimmer as I." Up to a point, this dualistic aspect can be constructive in making comparisons so that we can decide which items are more preferable and which actions will be most advantageous to our interests. However, since our thoughts usually operate on auto-pilot, with little conscious monitoring or direction from us, and since the prevailing tenor of verbal input from newspapers, radio, TV, and casual conversation is usually of a critical and complaining nature, the danger is that most of our thoughts will unconsciously tend toward setting up oppositions between ourselves and the rest of the world.

The majority of the stress and anguish we feel each day arises from the oppositions that we create in our minds. As we are on our way to work in the morning, we set up arguments and confrontations with co-workers and supervisors. In actuality, most of these confrontations never materialize. But that doesn't stop us from formulating a fresh set of mental arguments the next day. In almost every one of these dramas, we place ourselves at one end of the thought-line, as the hero, or victim. At the other pole is our opponent, the person who has criticized our work, given us too much to do, taken credit for our great idea, etc. You may disregard all these mental dramas as harmless daydreaming. But our thoughts have power. Each thought is a dynamic, energy charged vibration that does not simply pop into our heads and then disintegrate. Every thought we have emanates outward, like a signal from a radio transmitter. They interact with other signals and have real effects in the world. Just think of what happens when you press the button on a remote control device. A vibration issues forth, which may turn on your television, or raise or lower your garage door. The vibration of your thoughts is more subtle, yet it is just as powerful. Even more so.

We create machines, skyscrapers, and highways with our thoughts. We also create our relationships and, if we are not careful, destroy them with our thoughts. It requires persistent discipline to prevent the rational faculty from running on autopilot all the time, and most of us may be too preoccupied to monitor our thinking process continually and redirect it when it is not serving a constructive purpose. Still, it would be of great benefit to us to increase our awareness of how our thinking process operates. We need to be able to develop the mental agility to recognize when our rational faculty is setting up oppositions just to keep itself occupied.

We've all seen how this process works in numerous comical skits. One character will make an innocent remark, and a second character will misinterpret what was said and then fabricate in his or her mind a fantastical, imaginary scenario that confuses and disturbs all of the other characters in the play. For example, our protagonist may overhear his sister on the phone: "You say the old girl's in bad shape? I see... she won't last much longer." He thinks the doctor is on the phone, delivering the bad news that his mother is dying. But it's really the mechanic, saying that it's time to buy a new car. The protagonist then goes out of his way to cater to his mother and make her comfortable, only his fawning kindness, and solicitude irritate rather than please his mother, and his sudden concern with funeral arrangements causes the other characters to think that *he* is about to die. Other stories, based on the same premise, can work themselves out more melodramatically or tragically. What happens in each case is that the rational mind seizes upon a slim fragment of information and spins a full-blown, entirely untrue, story around it.

Now, examine your own thoughts. Can you see where you have taken a stray remark and built a whole story around it? It may have been something someone said about a co-worker, or a relative, or it may have been a comment on the radio about someone you've never met. The story could have some basis in fact, or it could be entirely imaginary. The first thing to notice about this story is how easy it was to build it up from essentially nothing. It required no great effort on your part; all you had to do was let your rational mind roll along. The next thing to notice is the polar nature of this story; it has a protagonist and an antagonist. They could be individuals or groups of people, but the nature of their relationship is one of contending forces. They are in opposition to each other. The rest of the story, which can be quite extensive and elaborate, involves various actions, strategies, and countermeasures enacted by both sides.

Actually, our lives are filled with stories. And, at its root, what is a story? It is the account of a struggle between opposing forces. Once the struggle has been resolved, the story is over. In the words that end virtually every fairy tale, "They all lived happily ever after." Living happily ever after implies that all oppositions have been resolved and unity has been restored. In this state of blissful cohesion, there is no further story to tell.

Many times, when we daydream, we engage in this process of allowing our minds to dream up stories. It may be a form of idle entertainment, especially if it is a rather dispassionate story, and we have not placed ourselves in it as one of the characters. Most of the time, however, the story is about us. We are the protagonist, and we are contending with an opponent. This person could be a real person with whom we have one or more issues in dispute. Or it could be an imaginary character dreamt up to represent a force in society with which we are at odds, be it the government, a business interest, or a social or civic group. Now, the story is imaginary, all the action is hypothetical, yet the nature of the opposition is an issue that has real significance for us. We have a personal interest in this story, and therefore, as it plays and replays on the movie screen of our mind, we respond emotionally. That is, we charge this story with our energy.

Look into your own mind and determine whether the charged energy you are projecting outward from your being is of a constructive or a contentious nature. Since you are engaged in this practice every day, it is important to understand the consequences and the effects it may have upon you. First, if one of these stories is about opposition with a specific person over a specific issue, and you replay this story in your mind several times a day, it is quite likely that this story will soon materialize as a physical argument or confrontation. Like a signal from a remote control device, day after day you are projecting the same energy pattern, and eventually this energy will accumulate and crystallize into physical reality.

I learned this lesson in a very dramatic fashion many years ago. There was a person who had wronged me and against whom I harbored a deep resentment. I seldom saw this person, but in my mind, over a period of many months, I constructed and repeatedly rehearsed a scene of confrontation between us. Finally, and inevitably, the confrontation materialized. This person literally appeared on my doorstep and we went toe to toe over the issue that divided us. This blowup led to the eventual resolution of the matter, but in the ensuing weeks I realized that the situation could have been worked out in a much less acrimonious fashion. It was the persistent intensity of my envisioning a contentious face-off that made the event come to pass the way it did.

According to the old saying, practice makes perfect. If you perform the same physical motions over and over, you will eventually become proficient in executing them, whether it is tying your shoes, carving a turkey, or playing the piano. There was a time when you did not know how to button a shirt or pull up a zipper. Through daily practice you mastered these actions so long ago that you now perform them unconsciously. The constant repetition of thought patterns works in a very similar fashion; you construct a pattern to channel energy in a specific direction. If you think, day after day, about a confrontation with a certain person, you are mapping out a pattern of energy that will inevitably lead you to an intersection where that confrontation will occur. There's an old saying which goes, "be careful what you wish for." That which you wish for is something that you desire intensely and consistently. Wishing is the constant stating and restating of that desire. Again, you are constructing an energy pattern that will direct your actions to a specific destination. In both cases, that of materializing a desire or a confrontation, there are always larger aspects of the situation that we do not know and therefore do not factor into our conception of how things will work out. In regard to obtaining the object of our desire, we usually find that it comes attached to certain flaws or obligations that diminish its appeal, hence the cautionary note to be careful when we wish for something.

Remember that our thoughts are one-dimensional, while this world and our living experiences in it are three-dimensional. Our one-dimensional thinking, by its very nature, always fails to comprehend the whole picture, or three-dimensional situation. In the case of a confrontation, it may have suited our ego to imagine a scene where we give someone a good piece of our mind. However, in the actual event, we may receive back a good piece of the *other* person's mind, and what they say to us may be quite piercing and painful. Also, our adversary may be stronger, and have more resources or more powerful allies than we have. A battle usually has a winner and a loser. When we mentally place ourselves into a conflict, we invariably picture ourselves as the victor. However, our thinking is entirely one-sided, from our own perspective. When the battle is joined, and the other side shows up in person, we may find ourselves overmatched, and instead of sweet success, we may have to endure that sour taste of defeat.

Most of the time, fortunately, our mental dramas do not translate into physical confrontations. Even still, be aware that each time we use our thoughts to set up an opposition in our minds, we are investing energy in a profitless enterprise. Consider a typical experience: the car in front of you is traveling slower than you want to go, and you cannot pass it. In your frustration you begin to set up an opposition between yourself and the driver ahead of you. Of course, you are the hero. Your cause is just; your family, your company, and the world at large stand to benefit from your expertise and ingenuity—provided you arrive at your meeting on time. Meanwhile, this sloth in front of you is the villain. Lazy and uncooperative, he is blocking the road ahead of you because it is his mission to thwart the purpose of the meeting, ruin your family's prosperity, and also destroy the world, for good measure. I know I've overstated things a bit in this example, but yet... When you're in such a situation, haven't you experienced this sudden surge of enmity toward a person you've never met? In the case of a slow driver, he's not out to ruin your day, starve your family, or destroy the world. For any number of reasons, he simply isn't driving as fast as you want to go. It's not like he's out there taking up the pavement because he wants to obstruct you. Just like you, he's got somewhere to go. He's got bills to pay, a job to do, and the same distaste for the rat race that you have. If you met at a party, you'd find he's a pretty decent fellow. He's not a monster, he's not an ogre, and he's not stupid. He's simply going slower than you want to go.

The next time you find yourself in such a situation, try this exercise. Imagine that this faceless, obstinate stranger is actually someone you care about very much. Also imagine that they're having car trouble, or that they just broke their wrist, and that they are moving as fast as it is possible for them to go. Dismantle your opposition and instead identify with them and their situation, and your irritation will melt away.

This transference from foe to friend occurred quite quickly for me once. I live in a small town, so one encounters one's neighbors and friends on the road quite often. One day, a car abruptly pulled out of a gas station in front of me. I was forced to slow down. It was no big deal, but all at once my mind seized upon the impropriety of the other driver's action, and I began to formulate an opposition between my virtuous driving and the reckless driver ahead of me. Then I recognized the car. The driver was a very dear friend of mine, a lady who was about ninety years old. My slight irritation was immediately replaced with feelings of concern for her safety. Instead of an opposition, I found myself identifying with her condition: a lack of lateral mobility in her neck to look both ways, faltering eyesight, reflexes that were not as sharp as they should be. Beneath and around all the oppositions that our linear mind constructs is the eternal sea of unity. Arching over all the tiny differences that separate one from another is the perpetual bond of Divine kinship.

As a counterpoint to the mental tendency to think in dualistic terms, we need to restore our ability for apprehending the world in a more unified way. We do this through our feelings, which are non-verbal and multi-dimensional.

The word *feelings* may be a bit confusing, because it is often associated with an outpouring of emotion. This is not my meaning. When we are in a highly emotional state, we have narrowed the focus of our consciousness down to a very small area, usually just ourselves. At such times our rational faculty is often working feverishly, replaying certain memories that reinforce and extend that emotional state. If anything, this activity only intensifies our oppositions and our sense of separation from the rest of the world.

To be sensitive to the world with our feelings, we instead open up our consciousness to all manner of inputs from the world at large. This process tends more toward dispassion than passion, in that dispassion is receptive to information from all directions, whereas passion closes down and restricts our awareness. When we cultivate a highly aware state of acute, yet calm, sensitivity, we will receive valid information as it resonates through our entire body—what are often called "gut impressions." These impressions are not rational, in that they do not require one to employ verbal, dualistic thinking to compare or contrast them with any other thing. Rather, they are whole, uncontested facts.

To establish a healthy balance between our feeling impressions and our rational thinking, it is good to cultivate the qualities of acknowledgment and acceptance. Through the practice of many years, we have developed the habit of mentally segregating and rejecting all those situations, events, and people that we regard as irritating, threatening, unpleasant, or disagreeable. In this way we are resisting their presence, even trying to deny their existence. Resistance requires energy, so this fruitless daily activity robs us of vitality that we could be directing toward more constructive pursuits.

Resistance and rejection are futile. Everything in this world *is*. Horrible events, irritating people, nasty weather, insects buzzing around our heads—all are part of this moment in time. They are here whether we personally approve of them and want them here or not. We are a participant in this grand scheme of things, but we are not the arbiter of what belongs here, and what should be discarded and thrown out. Everything belongs. When we acknowledge the presence of every person and thing in this world, and accept that it has a right to be here and a purpose to fulfill, we will begin to transcend the drawbacks of dualistic thinking.

Rational thinking has a definite place and function in human society. However, if you want to remove a good deal of stress and irritation from your life, and contribute to a lessening of hostility and misunderstandings in the society at large, remember this: Outside of our dualistic interpretation of the world, in which we tend to attach a friend or foe label to everything and everyone, the world simply is. There are opposing forces, but they are not enemies of each other. They are simply parts of the whole. Winter is not the enemy of summer, a glacier is not the enemy of a desert, vanilla is not the enemy of chocolate. Rather, they are partners in a dance. In our own lives, there are some dance partners with whom we will engage in struggle, while with other partners we will move gracefully in step. Despite the dissimilarities of our costumes, we are all dancers. And the music that animates one and all is the Divine energy of unity.

Acknowledgment and acceptance dissolve the tension of opposition. They put us back in touch with our earliest sensations and experiences in this world, which occurred before we acquired language and thinking. As such, our rational mental functions run on top of our visceral, feeling perceptions. Through attention and practice, we can establish a complementary balance between our dualistic thinking and our non-verbal, sensory awareness. In the next chapter we will explore techniques that will allow us to venture beyond the confining aspects of duality.

Chapter Five

You Choose Your Thoughts

In the previous chapter we discussed the tendency of linear thinking to frame our observations and relationships in terms of dualities. While this construct profoundly influences the way we interpret our experiences in this world, we have seen that it is only a partial picture of the way things really are. It is within our power, and indeed it is our birthright, to live more fully in this world. In this chapter we will explore a technique that will enable us to do so.

It is difficult, if not impossible, for a person to remember the early years when he or she was an embodied awareness with no thoughts. A baby knows no words and has not yet learned so much as to associate the sound of his name with himself. We can have consciousness and sense impressions without thoughts. However, from the moment of birth, we are surrounded by people who use words constantly to communicate their thoughts. Through daily exposure to these people and their persistent instruction, we also acquire language and begin to think.

Thinking is a learned activity. At this point in your life you have been doing it for so long that you can't imagine not doing it. Each day there are issues that require a decision on our part, and we will purposefully think these matters over; assessing the facts, factoring in our own goals and desires, estimating the likelihood of a favorable outcome, and then deciding on a course of action. Most of the time, though, our minds are not so constructively employed. Yet we think anyway. It is as if our thinking is an ongoing stream of words that is always flowing, whether we are consciously directing it or not. However, this ceaseless flow of words need not be an automatic activity.

One of the most powerful insights of my life simply dropped into my head one day. In four words, this is what it was: **You choose your thoughts.**

The implications of this little sentence were astounding. Like everyone else, I took thinking for granted. Thinking was something that just happened. And, frankly, thinking was quite enjoyable, because most of the time the star performer in my thoughts was me. Over a number of years I had periodically practiced meditative techniques wherein one temporarily empties one's mind of all thoughts. But this insight was a new challenge. For now I realized that I actually had the power to choose and direct every one of my thoughts.

Thoughts are free. We can think them all day long and no one is going to present us with a bill. They are also inexhaustible; we don't have to worry about depleting a resource that is in short supply. However, imagine for a moment that you actually did have to pay for every single thought you had. And the price was not cheap—let's say it cost one dollar per minute of thinking time. At that rate, ten hours of non-stop thinking would cost you six hundred dollars. If you had to pay six hundred dollars each day for your thoughts, you might start to look for ways to economize. You would ask, are all of those thoughts really necessary?

If you were to compile an inventory of each thought that you had over the course of one day, and then were to assign each thought to a category, what would that inventory reveal? To start, let's list some categories of thought. First would come daily decisions, thinking about what you're going to have for breakfast, what to wear to work, and what groceries you need at the store. The next category would be creative problem solving. You think about the proper placement for a new shelf in your closet, and exactly which fasteners and tools will be best suited for the job. Other problems to be solved could involve issues at work, timetables for getting projects finished, scheduling of meetings and appointments, and formulating budgets. A third category would be daydreaming: thinking about a trip abroad you would like to take, musing about performing perfectly in the sport of your choice, or dreaming about a romantic encounter.

You assign each one of your day's thoughts to the above categories and add them up. However, your total is way below the ten hours of thinking you did yesterday. You realize you missed a category. This one contains all the repetitious thoughts of a gossipy nature, like: Why did so-and-so say that to me... The next time I see him, I'll say such-and-such... No one appreciates how hard I work... if I were the boss, I'd... And on and on and on. When you look at the full tally, you see that, by a large margin, most of your thoughts fall into the final category. If you had to pay real money for these thoughts, would it be worth the price to entertain them?

Most of the time, we let our thinking faculty run without any constructive topic to think about. In this way, we do not have a firm purpose for our thoughts, and little snippets of gossip will spring up in response to the slightest stimulus. These thoughts will be influenced by the mood from without, since they are receiving no conscious direction from ourselves. What is the general tone of outside stimuli? Look at the way that stories are depicted in newspapers, and the general attitudes that are expressed over the radio and television, as well as the emotional flavor of what people around us are saying. The general tone is one of complaining, criticizing, and fixing blame. In general, it is soap opera. If we are not thinking constructively, the thinking process falls into the rhythm of the prevailing stream of words around us, and we wind up cycling and recycling gossipy, negative, melodramatic soap opera thoughts.

At this point it is fair to ask: Just whose thoughts *are* you thinking? Are they yours, generated by you to address a particular interest or issue in your life? Or do they originate outside yourself, and your brain takes them in like wayward travelers and gives them a home, even though they might spill things on the carpet and wreck the furniture? Stray thoughts, bits of gossip that the thinking faculty seizes upon and allows to cycle over and over again in your mind, are like parasites. Thoughts require energy. At the end of a day, when you're exhausted and ready to tumble into bed, you know you need to sleep. But which part of you really requires the rest, your body or your mind? Scientific tests have shown that muscles, even after a strenuous workout, need only a few minutes of rest to recharge, and then they are ready to work again. The most significant muscle in your body is your heart, and it never sleeps; it beats from the moment you're born until the moment you die. In between each beat, the heart does rest, but that resting phase only lasts a fraction of a second, and then it is ready to beat again. When we go to bed each night it is our minds that need several hours of time off to recharge properly. Experiments in sleep deprivation have shown that, when one is prevented from sleeping for a week or longer, mental and psychological problems of a long-term nature will result, while the body suffers no undue, or lasting, damage.

Thinking expends energy. Most of us are, at best, only vaguely aware of how much power our thoughts have. With our thoughts, we can bring new situations and material objects into being. If you allow your mind to idly spin out one pointless soap opera scenario after another all day long, you will be squandering vast amounts of real energy that you could be constructively channeling toward realizing your goals. Again, it is within your power to choose your thoughts, every minute of the day. If you do not exercise this choice and, instead, let all kinds of trivial thoughts hold sway in your mind, then what kind of an independent individual are you? Who's driving your bus? If you let your mind be filled with the gossipy thoughts of a co-worker or relative—or even some voice on the radio—you are tethered to them, like a slave. If your thoughts are not your own, neither is your life.

If you were to make a list of every single one of your thoughts for one day, how would you feel about having it published in the newspaper? Are you ready to admit publicly your ownership of all those complaining and mean spirited thoughts?

You choose your thoughts. At least, it is within your power to do so. Imagine going through a day where you did choose every one of your thoughts. You would choose the topic, begin thinking about it, come to a conclusion or decision, and move on to the next topic. When you had run through all of the topics that required thought for a decision or to solve a problem, you would then be free to daydream, or to cease thinking altogether, until the need arose again to exercise this faculty.

Choosing each individual thought can invigorate your life, increase your awareness and effectiveness, and open up doorways to profound insights and realizations. Of course, if you were to use your thinking faculty only when it was required to serve a positive purpose, you would find that there is quite a bit of time each day when you don't need to think at all.

Not think? At first, the rational faculty will recoil from the idea of an inactive, empty mind. Understand that the thinking process is almost an entity unto itself; it wants to be used and will immediately throw up a wall of fear against the prospect of being shut down. First is the fear of the unknown. Since you have been thinking nonstop for many years, you have identified your existence with thinking. In fact, much of our modern philosophy is founded on René Descartes' maxim, "I think, therefore I am." The implications of this maxim are potentially disastrous, for it implies that if you were to stop thinking, you might cease to be, and blink out of existence altogether. Or, even if you continued to exist, you might enter into some twilight realm where you wouldn't be able to restart the thinking process. Or, once restarted, it might be impaired from disuse, no longer able to serve you as effectively as before.

Fear not. You are eternal, and you have existed in non-thinking forms for eons. Thinking is a skill you acquire in this lifetime. Like a winter coat, it is something you can put on or take off without changing or diminishing the underlying entity that is you. The thinking faculty, moreover, is infinitely able. If you suspend thinking for a while, when you resume, your thought process will immediately be running at full speed and full strength. Imagine a rich seedbed of fertile, brown earth. It contains neither a pebble nor plant, just dark moist soil. Such is the quality of the empty mind. When the slightest speck of a seed lands on the surface, a full-sized plant immediately springs forth, branching out in all directions, sending forth luxuriant leaves and stems and flowers. The plant, in turn, begets an immediate forest of other plants, all mature in size and connected to each other in one vast web of pulsating growth. Such is the power of the thinking faculty to seize upon the slightest stimulus and to construct a whole network of interrelated thoughts. Its creative power is unimaginable, and the power is always there.

What is to be gained by not thinking? First, a quiet mind will conserve our mental energy so that we can direct it toward those issues and goals that really matter in life. Second, when the mind is deliberating over an issue, its dualistic tendency can split the topic into pros and cons, thus presenting opposing arguments in favor of at least two different ways to proceed. When the conscious mind is still, our deeper, non-verbal consciousness can then sort, order, and evaluate the arguments, thus making us aware of the alternative that is most consonant with our aims and needs.

Beyond these utilitarian benefits, not thinking will open up our awareness to the world around us, possibly giving us a glimpse into unseen realms. Picture a journey that you take every day, like going to school or work. You know the way by heart, but how much do you know about the landscape you are passing through? How many houses do you pass, what color are they, what architectural styles do they represent, and how are they landscaped? I'm not recommending that you become compulsive about noticing every detail, but there are house-sized objects that you have driven past every day for years and yet never seen. When your thinking faculty is zooming along at top speed, mulling a problem or replaying a soap opera that it has recited to you many times before, you are essentially blind to the world around you. Deaf, too. How many times in conversation have you become so engrossed in your own thoughts that you failed to hear what another person was saying? A quiet mind allows us to be more aware of our present circumstances. We will see more, hear more, and learn more.

When we think, we invariably remove ourselves from the present moment and either dwell in the past or project ourselves into the future. The only place that we really exist, however, is in the present, the eternal now moment. Many of our thoughts take us back to the past, and often the only purpose is to dwell on the disappointments, insults, and mishaps we have suffered. These events have happened already; we can't change them. By constantly revisiting them with the attitude of feeling sorry for ourselves, we are only retracing the unsuccessful patterns of our past behavior and forging them into the templates we will adhere to in the present and the future. What a waste of good living time.

Thinking out our plans for the future is a constructive exercise. However, let's be honest; many of the thoughts we project into the future are of the soap opera variety. We ponder what we will say or do to someone in retaliation for something he or she has said or done to us. Or we dredge up a sad scene from the past and spin out a future scene where once again we are the tragic, unappreciated, unloved figure. This is just another indulgence in feeling sorry for ourselves. But our thoughts do carry materializing energy. Is this sad scene we are envisioning something we really want to step into and experience again when that future moment becomes the physical present? Allowing our thinking faculty to lock us in the past or the future can be very emotionally wearing.

In contrast, when we are in the present, with a blank mind, we become caught up in what *is*. The present moment is neutral; only by thinking about it do we assign it a value and decide whether we like it or not. If we experience the present without bringing in the judgmental factor of thought, we are able to apprehend the world in an even-tempered, accepting way. The beauty of the most mundane objects will shine through; the underlying connectedness and meaning of every element in our surroundings will subtly impress itself upon us.

A quiet mind is also a passageway into the wider realms of the imagination. Without the interference of a lot of busy, buzzy, conscious thoughts, great visual, musical, and philosophical landscapes can reveal themselves. With our heightened perception we are able to discover hitherto unknown arrangements and combinations of matter and relationships. By suspending our thoughts, we open ourselves to a sea of infinite possibilities.

Most of the time we spend our lives seeing things and situations consistently in the same particular way because that is how our incessant thinking has always described them to us. But this oft-repeated description is just one exceedingly narrow interpretation of the vast, vital, multi-layered reality we inhabit. Whole realms of wonder are literally at our fingertips, within our sensory capabilities. They are invisible to us only because, through unbroken habit, we have become deafened and blinded by the roar and glare of our conscious thoughts.

Consider this possibility: Your thoughts actually produce a physical substance, a transparent film that is deposited wherever you go. Locations where you habitually spend time, such as your home and place of work, receive daily deposits of this transparent "thought stuff," which are like a series of plastic overlays. After a period of years, when you look at a room in your home or a portion of your workplace, you are looking through the accumulated overlays, which are colored with all the emotions and thoughts you have emitted in that space. You don't so much see the place, but rather the film of all the energy you have deposited there.

When we dispel the mental chatter, even for a fraction of a second, amazing impressions from the world around us can flood into our consciousness. There is a hackneyed saying that you can never go home again. This saying implies that, even if you return to the neighborhood and surroundings of your youth, you can never recapture the feeling and essence of your earlier years. As I see it, the dark film of all your mental overlays is what prevents you from going home again. If you could peel back the overlays, you would find the earlier reality is still there.

I had a profound confirmation of this fact several years ago when I returned to the house where I had grown up. My parents still lived there, and a large tree had fallen in the woods. I arrived with my chainsaw and worked intently for several hours, first cutting up all the branches and limbs, then sectioning the solid trunk into firewood-sized lengths. By the time I made the last cut, I was perspiring profusely and physically spent. I stood for a moment, gazing at all the work I had just completed, without thinking about anything in particular. After running the chainsaw almost nonstop for a few hours, the sudden silence was most welcome. Only it wasn't totally silent. Snatches of birdsong wafted into my ears. Also, beyond the aroma of the fresh cut wood, I was aware of the overall scent of the forest. The mineral content of the rocks and soil, and the corresponding smells that they emanated, differed significantly from the area where I now live.

While I had grown up and moved on, the same species of insects and birds still inhabited my old neighborhood. The scent of the soil, rocks, and vegetation was also the same. When I shut off the chainsaw, I was momentarily content with the work I had just finished and too exhausted to start thinking about what I would do next. For a short instant, I entertained no thoughts whatsoever. And a marvelous thing happened. Immersed in the unchanged sensory impressions of my early youth, I again glimpsed the world as I had when I was four years old. *I had gone home.* At that moment, I realized that each era and place in our lives is actually a persistent vibration that we can tune into at any time. The only trick is to suspend thinking. An empty mind allows us to peel back the overlays of all our subsequent thoughts, and to revisit any place or point in time.

How does one shut off the thinking process and silence the mind? It is both remarkably easy and exceedingly difficult to do. It is easy in that all one needs to do is decide to stop thinking, and then do so. It can also be difficult in that everything around us is a potential stimulus inviting us to think about it. As I mentioned earlier, the thinking process wants to be used, and it has a wide array of seductive wiles to keep us thinking. We derive great comfort from thinking about ways to make more money, win the love of a special person, acquire luxurious material possessions, be a heroic figure, and so on.

The first step in temporarily ceasing one's thoughts is realizing that there is something more profound, more rewarding, and more enjoyable beyond the realm of thinking. Once we form this conviction, we will put aside the pleasures and comforts of gossipy thinking because we want to experience something that is even better. In this way, we do not feel deprived or denied. We turn away from thinking because we have a greater desire to explore the territory of non-thinking.

Since the rational mind is so keen to be churning out thoughts all the time, many cultures have devised techniques to sort of trick the mind into suspending thought. Indian mantras are a series of syllables that do not connect to any rational items or issues. By repeating a mantra over and over, the mind becomes clogged with syllables that don't lead to other thoughts. The mind can only hold one thought at a time, and if that thought is a mantra that revolves around itself and makes no sense, the mind gradually ceases to think.

I have frequently used a similar technique by repeating to myself, "choose your thoughts, choose your thoughts." Or, simply, the word, "Choose." Any word or brief set of words or syllables will do. The idea is to calmly and gently disengage from thinking without alarming the mind. In this way, one remains awake and aware so that one can witness and experience sensations without attaching one's consciousness to any particular item and thinking about it. It's like being on a ride where you are entirely safe, yet you are moving through spectacular scenery so rapidly that all you can do is drink in all the marvelous sights and sounds without reflecting upon any of them.

Like acquiring any skill, one becomes more adept at quieting the mind with practice. In time, it will become unnecessary to use a gimmick because one's desire to experience the state of not thinking will far outweigh the mental invitations to keep recycling the same tired thought patterns.

To be sure, thinking is an essential activity we will engage in every day. However, by understanding that it is within our power to choose and direct every one of our thoughts, we will become more effective in pursuing our desires and goals, and more self-possessed, self-directed, and relaxed. We will be a thinker who employs thoughts for a useful purpose. But we will not allow our minds to be hijacked by stray gossipy thoughts and parasitic negative attitudes.

Chapter Six

Coming Here on Purpose

As long as humans have been on Earth, we have been asking, Who am I? and, What am I doing here? Some of us ask these questions more frequently and insistently than do others. And each one of us comes up with unique answers, which may be more or less satisfactory and comforting. In my own case, the answers keep evolving and expanding. While there was a single, cathartic moment when I fully realized that I am an eternal being, the period of preparation leading up to that moment, and the ensuing time it took to digest this insight and begin to incorporate it into my daily life, took nearly a year. The following year, a similar process unfolded as I grew into an awareness of my divine nature. And the next year, the big theme was unity. Although I now feel at home with these aspects of my being, understanding them in terms of this earthly life is an ongoing adventure. I'm learning new things all the time. As for duality—the tendency to split things into opposing factions and then take sides—I'll be wrestling with that issue for the rest of my life.

It is the aim of this book to identify and describe the qualities that serve as the stage or the landscape upon which we enact the mission of our lives. However, in this chapter I want to address an issue that bedevils me from time to time, one that has troubled and concerned everyone

I've met. Why is life so unfair and unkind? If we are all entities of divine goodness, why do such senselessly awful things happen to us?

Whenever we are on the verge of feeling overwhelmed by what seems to be the malevolent capriciousness of this insensitive world, it is good to remember that we are eternal. Hostile relationships, financial problems, war, pestilence, and disease will all pass, and we will remain intact. We did not have to come into this world; we chose to. If we look at our life from the perspective of our eternal natures, we will come to understand that we came here to deal with certain situations, participate in certain events, and engage in activities on this physical plane with certain entities. It's as if, when we are in a spiritual state, we design a travel itinerary on Earth, that goes through beautiful, sunny lands, as well as dangerous, stormy passes. Then we jump into a body and follow that itinerary.

Since we make the choice to enter into this world, you may fairly ask why so many people are impoverished and afflicted. It might be plausible that, here and there, an individual might choose a painful or difficult life. But why are so many people beset with such awful handicaps? It seems stupid that so many souls would purposely choose such difficult lives. From what I have been able to figure out, there are several factors at work here.

First, when you are in a spiritual dimension, prior to being born into this one, you are free from pain and stress. Consider the state you are in right now. If you are sitting comfortably, reading this book, and your body is not in any acute pain, it is difficult for you to imagine the intense suffering and incapacitation of a severe toothache or earache. You have probably experienced these afflictions in the past. But right now, when you are pain free, it is almost impossible to fully recall just how sharp and agonizing those pains were, and how you could barely think of anything except the pain. Eventually, the crisis was resolved. The infection passed; the tooth was repaired or extracted, and the agony you went through became a memory.

From the vantage point of a spiritual existence, the prospect of difficult situations in a physical life has less of an impact than your memory of a long ago toothache. When you are planning a life, your main concerns are the purpose for which you will live and the lessons you will learn from that living experience. Usually, it is through the most difficult and painful experiences that we learn the biggest lessons. Remember that you are a daring adventurer. At this moment you might not feel like one, and you may even look back over your life and concede that you have behaved more like a coward than a hero, seeking almost always to avoid painful situations and confrontations. But be assured that even a coward in this world is a brave soul. It takes a tremendous amount of courage to step out of the pure spiritual realms and take the plunge into physical existence. In fact, compared with the initial trauma of entering into a fragile, acutely sensitive body, all the other hardships of this physical life may appear to be minor.

Also, earthly life is a free-will dimension. We come here with a plan and a purpose. But this world is not a passive place where we are the only actor with an agenda and a will. This world is teeming with billions of other entities, each with its own plans and purposes, some of which may be at odds with our own. However, that is one of the challenges that we came here to face. We have a plan, and the agendas of others may assist or hinder us in carrying out what we have come here to do. Say, for instance, we came here to be an architect and we have a phenomenal vision for a complex of buildings where many people will be able to live and work in beauty, grace, and style. This complex will nurture and elevate the spirits of everyone who sets foot in it. We have been properly schooled, taken all the pertinent courses of study, and are licensed architects. We have a complete set of blueprints for our proposed complex. The buildings are beautiful, energy efficient, and financially feasible. Now the complications begin. Despite the excellence of our design, the economy is in a recession, many builders are facing bankruptcy, and the banks are not lending any money for new construction. Or, the economy may be in great shape, and we may have banks and builders eager to begin the project. But there are one or more groups, civic, environmental, or religious, who have objected strongly to the complex being built on the site we have chosen. The property has already been purchased, yet now we face months of hearings before planning boards, zoning boards, historical review boards, and environmental agencies. And then possibly years of litigation even if we do secure all of the permits and approvals. The project may never get built, although that was what we came into this life to do. As far as becoming an architect, we mastered all of the courses of study and technical skills, and fulfilled all of the requirements. If the project is turned down, has the purpose of our lives been thwarted? And therefore, has this whole life been a mistake?

No, for several reasons. First, as an architect, we are here to engage in a profession that will involve building and designing many projects. Some will get built, and some will not. Bear in mind that creativity is infinite, while this physical world is bounded and finite. In nature, each species has a reproductive potential many, many times greater than that which is necessary to continue the species. For example, if each one of the spores in a single giant puffball were to grow to full size, all of those billions of puffballs would take up a space greater than the size of the Earth. In the case of a building project that is never built, many benefits may sprout from this supposed failure. Elements of its design and innovations that it elicited from our imagination may be incorporated into other projects. Also, sometimes a setback can be very therapeutic in that it may rein in our egos and teach us to be more sensitive to the concerns and input of others. Just because our life does not go entirely according to our plan does not mean that it was a mistake or that it was not worth living. Remember, there is value in everything, even thwarted plans. Nothing is wasted.

But let's look at a more difficult case—someone who is born deformed, or with a chronic congenital disease. Why would anyone willingly choose to enter into such a life? It may sound trite to say that it is for the challenge of experiencing such a life. But consider that our rational way of evaluating living conditions and quality of life is the most superficial way of comprehending what is actually going on. Because of the limitations imposed by someone's affliction or handicap, that person is often able to open his or her awareness to aspects of physical life that normally endowed people do not perceive. They may see, hear, or comprehend elements of this world and of the human condition with a deeper and richer understanding than do the rest of us. Consider that Ludwig van Beethoven wrote sublimely beautiful and majestically moving music when he was totally deaf. Also, and this is no small issue, a person with a severe handicap provides an opportunity to his family and others to develop and extend their qualities of patience, compassion, and acceptance in ways they would not have done if the person had been born with normal attributes. Many times the parents of a disabled child have said that this child made them finer people, and taught them the meaning of unconditional love.

When we are in this life, it is common to think that this is all there is, that our brief stay on this small planet represents the whole of our existence. But from the perspective of the spiritual realm, we see that each physical life is but a short episode in our eternal existence. From the spiritual viewpoint, knowing that each earthly life is a very temporary affair, it is a lot easier to make the choice to endure a life in difficult or deprived circumstances, for the benefit of finding out what it is like.

From your present frame of reference, consider a movie you have seen recently where you strongly identified with one of the characters. You were very much moved by the plight of that character, and after the movie was over you continued to dwell on the issues the character had to face, and how you would have responded if you had been in her place. That night you may have elaborated on the movie in your dreams, and for days afterward you continue to ruminate on the decisions the character made and how she pursued her relationships. All the while, you imagine how you would have acted, how you would have dealt with the other characters, and how the whole story would have turned out differently, and better, if you had been that character.

Do you see what you are doing? You are creating a whole life, and a mission for yourself. It's all an extended daydream, of course. Or is it? Imagine that you were outside of physical reality, and you were to fashion such a compelling drama, and then enter a body to act it out. The character that you have identified with is persecuted, exploited, and betrayed. She has an extremely difficult and painful life. Yet, at the same time, the struggle of this life is a very appealing one, for it is an heroic endeavor from beginning to end. In the spiritual realm you know that no matter what happens to you in this earthly life, the persecution, alienation, and suffering will have no ill effect on your soul. The whole life is but a role that you take on, just like the actor in the movie, to perform as best as you can.

Before we are born, our soul knows it is eternal and cannot be harmed, and that everything it encounters in this lifetime—joy, sorrow, pain, ecstasy—is for the benefit of the experience. Remember that there is a much larger picture than the one we see from within our human bodies. It isn't that some people have particularly difficult lives because God is indifferent or some demon holds sway over the Earth. For a variety of purposes, we enter this world with all kinds of talents and handicaps, to act out an enormously wide range of roles.

Consider that you came into this life *on purpose,* to live the life you are living. Much of the time, due to fear of pain, embarrassment, or unpleasantness, we try to evade or avoid the very experiences we came here to have. I have found one simple practice to be of great benefit. You can employ this technique every day, or at those times when you are confronted with a situation that is particularly challenging or potentially disastrous. Say to yourself: *I came into this life to live this day.* However pleasant or harrowing the upcoming event may be, you came into this life for the purpose of engaging in this specific activity and getting to experience this situation from the inside, in all its nerve-tingling splendor. So keep your eyes open, take in every bit of the experience, and play your part for all you're worth. In triumph or failure, you're going to come through it and be whole on the other side.

I'll make this point several times in these pages. You are in this life for the experience. This world is indifferent with respect to whether you get treated fairly or not, or are properly rewarded for all your work and effort. The real reward is living fully, knowing the pure exhilaration of expressing your being without reservation, unconcerned with victory or defeat.

Chapter Seven
The Truth Always Outs

It is a common practice for people to put the best face on things. We all make a living by selling something—goods, services, sweaty labor—to others. It is necessary for our own survival that we are able to sell what we are offering. And the marketplace is crowded with competitors. Everyone else is selling whatever they can, and many of them are selling the same thing that we are; be it pumpkins, accounting expertise, or the manual strength and skill of their muscles. So we toot our own horn to let people know that what we are offering is of great quality, and they won't be disappointed. We advertise. And maybe we exaggerate a little.

This tendency extends beyond the marketplace to stretch across the entire web of our relationships. We want people to like us. So we may pretend to share the same deep devotion to the political causes, hobbies, or sports teams that they favor. To be accepted, we may eat things that don't appeal to us, drink and smoke things that we either didn't want in the first place, or in amounts that we know are unwise and unhealthy. With regard to our romantic interest in another person, we will do our best to paint a glowing, if not quite accurate, picture of our physical prowess, our intellectual gifts, our past achievements, the importance of our job, our age, our income, and our future prospects. We're not exactly lying—certainly we don't believe we are—we're simply embellishing the truth a little.

As the behavior of the individual has a direct influence on the workings of society, we see the same practices being employed by companies, government agencies and politicians, and nation states. Sometimes the claims made for a product are overstatements: you take Acme vitamins but feel no new surge in energy, you buy a certain brand of toothpaste or drive a certain model of car, yet it does nothing to enhance your attractiveness to the opposite sex.

Many of these exaggerations and misstatements, fibs though they may be, are harmless enough. But the practice goes much further, to the point where lies are presented as truth, or the truth is covered over, even denied. Examples of such disregard for and denial of the truth are all around us. A company will sell a product containing substances that poison and debilitate its customers, all the while claiming that the product is perfectly safe. Officers of another company will issue false financial statements claiming the company is prospering, while at the same time selling their shares in advance of the company's collapse. Throughout the ages, governments have promoted hundreds of versions of the Big Lie. Some examples are propaganda designed to arouse the citizenry's enmity for another nation, of even to persecute a segment of its own population. Policies to benefit the privileged few will be trumpeted as fostering the welfare of everyone. Confiscation, suppression of dissent, graft, and military atrocities will be denied outright. For thousands of years, billions of people, in every nation on Earth, have been oppressed, tortured, and cheated out of their divinely authorized birthright to live a free and productive life, all the while being told by their oppressors that the government is kind and just, and that the squalid, repressive conditions are really for their own good.

Abraham Lincoln stated, "You can fool all the people some of the time, and some of the people all the time, but you can not fool all the people all of the time." My grandmother had a more pithy expression: **The truth always outs.**

I remember nodding in agreement whenever she would say this phrase and smiling inwardly at the slightly comical tone in which she uttered it. Over the years, though, I observed how uncannily accurate this saying was. Sooner or later, the truth of each matter and event will ultimately and inevitably be revealed.

This maxim applies universally. Whether it is the identity of someone who committed a murder eighty years ago, an account of what a politician knew about a particular scandal, when he knew about it, and the extent of his own involvement in it, or the comparatively trivial information concerning who smashed your pumpkin last Halloween, the truth will become known.

How does this principle work? On the most superficial level, you could ascribe it to the human tendency to talk. Even when they have not done something particularly praiseworthy, people will mention it. Sometimes a criminal will disclose details concerning his crime because he's motivated by a desire to brag, especially since the authorities are baffled and he seems to have gotten away scot-free. Even when someone has done something reprehensible, there is still an inner prompting to claim credit for the deed. Actions, in and of themselves, are something that so captivate the human mind that we are possessed with an almost undeniable urge to discuss them, no matter how antisocial or depraved they may be.

In the realm of corporate or political affairs, the principle applies to an even greater degree. Here, in almost all instances, more than one person is involved in a misdeed. Several people may have been involved, but most of them in minor roles, so they do not feel a high level of guilt for what they have done. There is also the insecurity factor. Each person is involved to a different degree, and almost everyone has an incomplete picture of the whole affair, so there are loose ends, information that they do not have, which is therefore out of their control. Such information may be used against them. Many times a participant in a scandal will break under the pressure of this uncertainty, cooperate with the authorities, and turn in the others who were involved, before one of them turns him in.

Yes, people will talk. But the issue goes much deeper. The reason that the truth always outs is because the truth is an independent, indestructible thing in and of itself. That which exists, be it a physical object or an event, *is*. It exists independently of you and me and everyone else. And everything that exists is knowable. It has a persistent resonance that can be tuned into, in the same way that you can pick up a frequency from a radio station when you adjust your tuner to a specific vibration. Earlier I mentioned that the vibrations of our thoughts and emotions will persist way beyond our earthly lifetimes. Some scientists have stated that the vibrations of every sound that was ever created are still reverberating around the universe. In the same way, the vibration of every action and event continues to exist indefinitely. The truth of everything is all around us. People can deny it and ignore it, sometimes for many years. But no one can annihilate it. The truth persists, for eternity.

We have all witnessed situations where someone has tried to conceal the truth, and the only person he has truly deceived is himself, for everyone else already knew the real situation. If anything, it was a big joke. The person acted and was regarded as a buffoon; everyone laughed and gossiped about his deceptive folly behind his back. We see these scenarios enacted frequently in plays and movies, as well as everyday real life. A company boss or government leader will pronounce the official lie, and all the underlings will shake their heads in agreement. However, as soon as the boss leaves the room, the underlings exchange knowing glances and sarcastic remarks. The organization goes to great effort to project a false picture, yet no one is being fooled. Within your own town or neighborhood, you can observe instances where a person will attempt to cheat or deceive others. This person may be successful for a while, but eventually the word will be out, and henceforth the deceptive person will be shunned. They won't be expelled from society entirely, but everyone who deals with this person will be cautious and distrustful, treating the person with extreme wariness. At this point, the cheater is the only one being fooled, for he still thinks that people trust him and believe his lies.

The truth about your character and virtue has a life of its own, and it's known as your reputation. All of your deeds, valiant and dastardly, are recorded upon it. Your reputation is a reflection of what is. If you feel that you deserve to be regarded more highly than you presently are, the place to begin making changes is within yourself. This is a dynamic system. You can't undo what has already been done, but the opportunity for redemption is as close as your next action.

The almost irresistible desire for people to talk and spill the beans, even when it is within their immediate interest to remain quiet, is directly tied to this indestructible quality of the truth. Fifty years after someone has committed a crime, the reality of that misdeed is still with them. Not just in their memory, but pulsing independently in the subtle, spiritual regions that interpenetrate this world. It has long been said that our misdeeds rest uneasily upon our conscience like an uncomfortable burden. There is no way to wipe them out of existence. The only way to remedy the situation is to own up to what we have done.

As long as we deny the truth, we are handicapping ourselves, because we are fighting the universe, trying to deny the existence of something which is. This ongoing act of resistance requires a great deal of energy. Look around you, at all the people who complain of feeling tired all the time. Could it be that each one of us, to a greater or lesser extent, is wearing himself out with the constant daily strain of denying and suppressing a wide range of truths and facts? How do *you* feel?

There is a timeworn saying from the Bible that the truth will set you free. Think about one particular truth that you have been trying to keep in the closet and maintain as a secret. Look at all the effort and energy you have devoted to its concealment. Now, imagine dropping your resistance, letting the truth out, and going on with your life. Forget for a moment what the consequences might be, for they will be temporary.

So many times, our fear of unpleasant outcomes inhibits us from moving forward. With respect to owning up to a past misdeed, we fear that the consequent penalty and punishment will be more than we will be able to bear. Whenever fear immobilizes you, *remember your eternal nature.* You will survive all penalties and punishments. By atoning for your misdeeds, trivial or grievous, you will finally put them behind you—no longer tethered to them.

We may also try to cover up the truth because we are afraid of what people might think of us if our foibles come to light. Bear in mind that our thinking process moves rapidly from topic to topic. When there is a mystery, the tendency is to dwell upon that one topic and speculate upon the answer. Once the truth is revealed and is out in the open, our curiosity is satisfied and our attention moves on to other topics. With respect to owning up to your own imperfect actions, people will quickly move on and devote their attention to other concerns.

One of the big issues when I was in college was the students' proposal to evaluate all the teachers and publish the results. Many of the faculty were vehemently opposed to this plan. One of my professors, though, strongly supported it. "Let's face it," he said. "nothing travels faster around this campus than a teacher's reputation." He realized that publishing teacher evaluations might not only set the record straight, but also spare the students a lot of distracting gossip and speculation.

Once you align yourself with the truth, with what is, you align yourself with the true flow of energy in the universe. Instead of wearing yourself out resisting something that you can never fully hide or defeat, you will once again be free to move forward energetically. We all marvel at the almost inexhaustible energy of little children. Our natural state in this world is to be full of energy. If we start out in such a high energy state as children, when our bodies require a great deal of energy to keep growing and developing, why is it that, when we have become adults and our bodies are fully grown, we are so tired? If anything, we should have more energy than a child. However, in early childhood, we have not yet developed the rational practices of concealing and resisting the truth. We frequently describe little children, in humor and dismay, as being brutally honest. That honesty, an acceptance and acknowledgment of what is, aligns children with the energetic flow of this world, so they are invigorated and vitalized all day long. Wouldn't you like to share in this state—actually return to it—once more?

If you try to deny the truth, you are resisting reality. Such an endeavor is futile, for we are encompassed by reality. There is no way that we can box it up and hide it away. It's like trying to lock all of the air in a building into one room. You can slam the door, seal it, barricade it, and secure it with a dozen locks. However, the air is still present on both sides of the door. Some people may think that, if they can hide or destroy sensitive documents or other incriminating evidence, the truth will never become known. But the truth exists independently of all physical objects. And it isn't located in a specific repository. The truth, all truth, exists everywhere. And it can be accessed everywhere.

I know this statement may sound farfetched. However, in recent years technology has devised *holograms,* which exhibit this very property. A hologram is an interference pattern that contains information. If you took a handful of pebbles and threw them into a pond, the resultant lacework of interpenetrating ripples would convey all the information about where and when each pebble dropped into the water. Holograms are produced by lasers. A pair of lasers will scan an object and trace an interference pattern on paper containing all the information about that object. A third laser then reads that interference pattern and translates it back into a picture of the original object. Let's say that the object is an apple. We scan the apple with lasers and produce a hologram on an 8-by10-inch piece of paper. To our eyes, the hologram is a meaningless mass of squiggly lines. But when it is read with a third laser—voila—we have an 8-by10-inch picture of our apple. What do you suppose would happen if that hologram were cut in half? Would each portion now reveal only half of the apple? Astonishingly, no. When the third laser reads each piece of the original hologram, it reveals the complete apple, half the size of the original. If the hologram were cut into a hundred pieces, each one of them would still display the entire apple, reduced in size. What's going on here?

In a hologram, the interference pattern contains all the information about the object it depicts at every point in the hologram. I know it sounds mind boggling, but that's how it works. All information resides everywhere. Researchers have found that our brains function holographically. Many of our memories are not located in one specific spot in the brain but can actually be accessed from multiple locations.

In the same way, all knowledge, and the ripples of all events that have ever occurred, persist and vibrate at all locations. For thousands of years, there has been a discipline known as divining, or dowsing, that is employed to discern the truth, and to recover knowledge that is needed but not physically apparent. The most common use of divining today is for locating underground sources of water, a substance that is universally needed.

A water dowser usually employs one or more variously shaped implements known as dowsing rods. When he passes over a vein of water in the ground, the rods will move in a discernible way. Modern science has speculated and debated for years over exactly what physical phenomena are responsible for this dowsing response. Some theorize that the water emits some kind of electromagnetic radiation that stimulates a reaction in the muscles of the dowser, and that causes the rods to move. However, one does not have to be standing directly above the water to determine its location. There are many cases on record of dowsers, sitting at home, going over a map of a distant property. With pinpoint accuracy they have marked a spot on the map and have given exact measurements from onsite landmarks, to show where to drill for water.

They will even say how far the vein is under ground, and how many gallons per minute it will produce. Water is not the only substance that can be located in this way. Minerals, oil, and lost objects are just a few of the other things that can be found with this method.

How? According to the principle that the truth always outs, that which is real and true vibrates continuously. Using the model of the hologram, all truth and all knowledge are present everywhere in the universe. Each true thing emits a persistent vibration. All a person needs to do is tune into that specific vibration and, like picking up the signal from your favorite radio station, that knowledge or information will come forth.

Beyond tuning into the truth in this way, there is another method that virtually everyone has used at least once in his or her life: intuition. Within each one of us, there is a direct channel to all knowledge and truth. For most of us, this channel gets clogged and covered up by the constant chatter of our rational minds. The truth is always there, but it is quiet. Unlike the people and enterprises around us, it has no need to advertise or call attention to itself. It simply *is*. To access this limitless realm of knowledge and truth, we need something that we rarely possess, a quiet mind. Each of us has at least some quiet moments. Sometimes they come to us in a time of relaxation and serenity. At other times, in moments of danger or extreme stress, the intensity of that instant can squeeze all thoughts out of our mind so that the true and proper course of action becomes immediately clear to us. The answer just manifests in front of us, whereas, especially in our agitated and stressed state, we never would have been able to think our way into it.

Divining may be described as applied intuition. You begin with a focused intention to discern a specific portion of the truth, quiet the mind, and then proceed in a methodical, step-by-step manner to bring that truth to light. When you tap into your intuition, you can receive a coherent picture, a vision, all at once. Many people will describe a profound intuitive experience as one in which they have heard or seen words and sentences that were pertinent to an important issue in their lives. In the same way, a whole picture or scene can be visually presented to you. It usually happens in a flash, and there is a deep, calm knowing within you that what you have heard or glimpsed is the truth. It may have to do with the past, in that you now have a full understanding of a past experience or relationship. Or it may be an insight into the true nature of a present situation. Or the intuition may deal with the future, perhaps as a warning of a danger you are going to encounter unless you alter your present course. Or you may receive a picture of the proper choices and actions to take to attain your goals.

Intuition connects us to our inner knowing. The truth is always there to be known, because it has an indestructible persistence all its own. When we live in accordance with the truth, we align ourselves with the flow of energy in the universe. We become invigorated and enlightened by it. Each time we try to conceal the truth, or reject and deny what is, we are pouring our energy into a futile exercise. We might as well be trying to dislodge the Earth from its orbital path around the sun. *The truth always outs* because there is no way to box it in. To live in the truth is to know freedom, and the boundless energy that accompanies it.

Chapter Eight

The Cyclical Nature of Physical Reality

Most of us consciously seek self-improvement. If we have a trade or profession, we periodically enroll in seminars and training classes to learn new techniques and keep abreast of new developments in our field of work. We may also expend regular effort in physical exercise to keep our bodies supple and healthy. By droves we enroll in continuing education classes and self-help workshops, and buy books, tapes, or CDs to instruct us in meditation, foreign languages, gourmet cooking, and so on.

Somewhere in your mind is a vision of yourself as a fully realized and perfected being, in this lifetime. For those who are serious about this quest, there is a destination, which we hope to attain within a year or so, when we will have gotten our act together, paid our bills, solved all our major problems, and are ready to sail on the calm waters of living happily ever after. Most of us have this picture. In it, we are at our ideal weight; we have learned everything we need to know to be successful for the rest of our lives; all of our relationships are loving, supportive, and fun; all of our health ailments have been cured; and we will never become angry, upset, or depressed again.

Sounds lovely, doesn't it? And it is certainly a state worth striving for. However, you're not likely to find it in this world. I'm not saying you should stop striving, because self-improvement is a big part of the reason we came into this world. But many people work and work, only to fall short of attaining their lofty vision. They then become discouraged and think that they are total failures. The flaw is not in them or their aspirations, it is in the vision of static perfection.

You're going to have good days and bad days. That's how the world works. A number of years ago I had the great good fortune to be at a lecture given by a remarkable healer. The man was a medical doctor and had run a holistic healing center for more than thirty years. He was a living testimony to healthy living; he was so vibrant and vigorous that my friends and I thought he was maybe sixty years old. At the end of his talk we were shocked to learn he was eighty. One would think that he had learned how to do everything right—the correct foods, proper exercise and outlook—and that he had attained the plateau of perfect health. Yet, during his lecture, he informed us that five years earlier, at the age of seventy-five, he had contracted an illness so severe that he thought it would end his life. When he recovered, he realized that until the age of seventy-five, he had not learned enough to understand and accept the lesson that this illness taught him.

One of the characteristics of the rational mind is the tendency to form static, unchanging pictures of how we want things to be. Our fundamental essence, our soul, is eternal and ageless. But this physical world we are visiting is a dynamic setting where all forms and situations are constantly changing. It might be helpful to look a little deeper into how physical reality is organized and operates. What follows is far from being the last word on the subject, but it may explain some of the issues with which we all wrestle.

We will begin with the circle. When it comes to the physical dimension, I believe the fundamental organizing principle is the circle. For many cultures all over the world, this shape has come to represent divinity and perfection. A circle has no beginning and no end. It is absolutely symmetrical and faces equally in all directions. For a given length of a perimeter, you can enclose more space inside a circle than you can in any other shape, so it is the paragon of efficiency.

From the flat, two-dimensional representation of a circle on a piece of paper, extend the circle into three dimensions, and you will have a sphere. Of all three-dimensional shapes, a sphere will contain the greatest volume within a given surface area. The sphere is also perfectly balanced, and possesses the greatest structural stability. Interestingly, when particles of matter in space come together and coalesce into stars, planets, and moons, they all take the shape of spheres.

Now, consider a four dimensional representation of a circle, where the fourth dimension is time. As we move through time, how could that motion be expressed in circular terms? Imagine a circular clock face. We will begin at the nine o'clock position, move up to the twelve, and then down to the three. At this point, we encounter a snag, because moving from three to four would imply moving backwards in time; and, in our experience of this world, time moves in one direction only. In order to keep moving forward, we will place a second circular clock face beside the first one, so that the three on the first circle adjoins the nine on the second circle. From the nine on the second circle, we move down to the six, and then up to the three, completing one full circle while always moving forward in time. Once we have done so, what does that circle look like? We have a line that first moves up, then down, then up again. If we continued to trace more circles through time, this line would continue to move up and down, up and down. Each up and down motion is called a cycle. *This is the essential principle of action in the physical, time-bounded dimension. It fluctuates, forming cycles.*

All actions in time will exhibit these rhythmic fluctuations. Each day it becomes light, and then dark at night. Over the course of the year, we pass through seasons that are alternately warm and cold. The moon waxes and wanes. The tides ebb and flow. The heart expands and contracts. Various machine parts move up and down, back and forth. A stream of water moving through an essentially flat landscape will not flow in a straight line, but snake back and forth in loops. Populations of insects and wild animals will show patterns of increase and decrease, as will prices of stocks, bonds, and commodities in the financial markets.

And what about yourself? Don't you have your good days and your bad days? On some mornings you will have a smile for everyone, while on other days every little thing seems to annoy you. There are times when everyone cooperates with you and endorses your ideas. Then there are times when you are frustrated at every turn. As the saying goes, you win some, you lose some. This phrase is usually uttered in resignation after someone has lived for several decades and experienced a good measure of victories and defeats. These ups and downs are not just the way of human society; they're the way of the whole physical universe.

Every speck of matter vibrates. What are these vibrations but up and down, back and forth motions, the hallmark of activity occurring in time? Due to the linear nature of our thinking, we tend to project whatever we are presently experiencing into the future with no variation. If we are happy now, we think that we have got the world figured out, and we will remain happy forever. If we are sad or discouraged right now, we can't see how our situation will ever change, and we are convinced we will never smile again. On both counts, we are wrong. Two other ancient sayings to keep in mind: What a difference a day makes. This too shall pass. Action through time moves up and down, and our moods, our luck, and our energy will also have peaks and valleys.

We frequently paraphrase a line from Robert Burns and say, the best laid schemes of mice and men often go astray. On a piece of paper, draw an undulating sine wave, which represents the curved trajectory of action through time. Now place a ruler, which represents our linear thinking, at any spot on this curved line. You will notice that our straight-line thoughts will always *run off at tangents* to the curved course of action. Hence our plans often stray from the path we have laid out for them.

What we need to do to make life easier on ourselves is to become more flexible in our attitudes, to "bend" our thinking. Of course, thinking can't help but be straight-line linear, so the only way to temper it with a broader perspective is to incorporate more input from our heart. For the sake of this discussion, let's say that the mind knows and the heart understands. It is with our understanding that we can bend our mental concepts around corners, and appreciate the three-dimensional curvature of action through time, instead of following our thoughts straight out over the horizon.

Also, our hearts lead us into areas where our minds would never allow us to go. Our rational thinking plots our actions along a straight line to a specific outcome, which it has determined is not only desirable, but also the only outcome that is acceptable. Our heart, however, will lead us into back streets and detours, which may make our journey more thrilling, messy, and complicated. This path of the heart will usually produce a different, yet more expansive and fulfilling, outcome than the one our rational thinking had anticipated.

Being open to the fluctuations of life will make us more nimble and adaptable. And happy. There is an uncertainty about this world, in that all situations are evolving out of a limitless number of possible outcomes. We see and think in straight lines, yet action forever takes a curved path, bringing up changes that were unforeseen and unplanned for. Yet, that's part of the charm of this world. We're here for the ride, and what a bore it would be if we could see the whole course in advance and not have any surprises. So welcome the unanticipated. It's part of this dimension's grand design.

There is one more way in which circles are profoundly expressed in physical reality. If you move through a circle in time and space, you will have a spiral. This pattern pervades the natural world. If you look down upon a spruce tree from above, you will see that the branches on the trunk are arranged in a spiral formation. The screws and bolts that hold together most of our buildings and machines are spirals. In fact, the DNA that contains the genetic code for all animals and plants in this world takes the form of two intertwined spirals, known as a double helix.

A spiral in motion is called a vortex, and the vortex lies at the heart of energetic, dynamic physical systems. When a seed sprouts and rises from the earth, it does not grow in a straight line. Time lapse photography shows that it spirals upward like a graceful dancer. Likewise, falling leaves and snowflakes trace out variously shaped spirals on their descent to the ground. Many of the properties of the vortex are still inexplicable to us. The vortex contains great power and energy, just think of a tornado. In eastern philosophy, highly charged vortices of energy, called chakras, are present in our bodies and serve as conduits through which vital energy from more subtle planes of existence charge and invigorate our bodies.

Indeed, our bodies display vortices in numerous ways. Just look at your fingerprints, or the pattern in which hair grows on your head. Your ear canal takes the shape of a spiral. And consider your very breath. From your nose to your lungs is a distance of only two feet. When you inhale, for the air to be properly utilized by your lungs, it must be warmed to your body temperature, filtered and cleaned of impurities, and humidified, so that it will not dry out and damage the sensitive, moist tissues of your lungs. How are these tasks accomplished in just two feet and the mere second and a half it takes to draw a breath? When you inhale, the air circulates through your nose and bronchial passages not in a straight line, but through multiple tiny vortices. On these circular pathways, each molecule of air comes into repeated contact with our nasal and bronchial tissues, which warm and moisten it, while also filtering out impurities and toxins. The journey through all these spirals is a lot longer than two feet, and when the air reaches the lungs it is warm, moist, and clean—and ready for the lungs to use it effectively.

The weather systems that bring us rain and fair weather are gigantic vortices of circulating air and moisture. Interestingly, when the circulation pattern is in a clockwise direction, this vortex is characterized by high barometric pressure and sunny skies. When the circulation pattern is counter-clockwise, the vortex produces low barometric pressure, clouds, and rain. This pattern is not unique to Earth. With our telescopes we can see vortices on the planet Jupiter. One of them, the Giant Red Spot, has been observed for more than three hundred years, and is larger than Earth itself. On a still larger scale, galaxies, which are composed of tens of billions of stars, are also spinning vortices. In fact, if you placed a satellite photograph of a hurricane next to a telescopic photo of a galaxy, they would look virtually identical.

Most of the technical progress we have made in this world, in harnessing energy and motion, derives from our use of the circle. What is universally acknowledged as the greatest invention of all time? The wheel, which is a circle. Electricity and telecommunications are based on cyclical fluctuations that result from action taking place in time. So far we have only penetrated the surface of the potential of the vortex. We live within a vast array of rhythms. Some are very noticeable to us, like the cycles of day and night, and the seasons. Others are more subtle, yet still discernible, like temperature variations within our bodies and the way the moon affects the tides and plant growth. Most rhythms, however, do not intrude dramatically into our consciousness. By cultivating awareness and understanding we will gain a better grasp of the fluctuations of our moods and fortunes. The more we realize that the course of our lives will carry us to many peaks and valleys, the more we can accept this world, enjoying the limitless variety it has to offer.

Chapter Nine
Having It Made

In the previous chapter I described the up and down, give and take nature of action in this world. These fluctuations of increase and decrease, expansion and contraction, grow directly out of the circular perfection of the physical plane of existence. I know it's not easy to welcome unanticipated alterations to our plans. It requires some ongoing effort to remain mindful that our plans and expectations, which we have projected in straight lines, will forever be straying from the curved course that action naturally takes. In this chapter we're going to explore another facet of this issue.

This is a beautiful and enticing world, and we possess a limitless creative capacity to fashion ingenious devices and beautiful objects from its native materials. We are also brilliant, vivacious, radiant beings, and the possibilities for exciting and stimulating interactions with our fellow adventurers, as well as for satisfying loving relationships, are also boundless. Of course, our imaginations far outpace our plodding physical bodies. In less than a second we can envision a work of art or a structure that will take months, even years, to bring into physical manifestation. We learn that it takes time and effort, not to mention money, to actualize those marvelous visions that so readily appear in our mind's eye. Still, these mental pictures are compelling, inspiring, and beguiling. And each one of us, according to our tastes and desires, holds certain enduring pictures in our minds—of an ideal home, a soul mate, a fashionable wardrobe, and so on.

These items of desire that we persistently envision merge into an overall picture that comprises our conception of a full and happy life. This is life as it ought to be—and life as we plan to live it—once we have developed the right personal relationships and acquired all the material objects that we need. We enjoy dreaming of that golden day when every element of our ideal life is in place. At that time there will be nothing left to acquire, no further fields to conquer, nothing else to strive for. We will have attained our goal, the battle will be won, and we can live out our days in peace and contentment. At that point, we've got it made.

What is irksome to us is that, even though we may work diligently year after year and pay our dues, the rewards we feel entitled to, the big payoff, has not materialized for us. What's worse, we notice that other people seem to have succeeded where we have failed.

Just look at the neighbors. The Smiths have a grand yacht. The Joneses take one great vacation after another. John Doe receives promotions regularly. And then there are the celebrities and star athletes, who make millions of dollars each year and bask in fame and acclaim. We're still struggling, while all those folks have got it made. And we're just as good and deserving as they are.

We haven't given up on our dream. Each week we buy our lottery tickets, and we fantasize about making a killing in the stock market or perhaps having a phenomenally lucky day at the races or in a casino. We keep telling ourselves, all we need is one big break; then we'll have it made. If we just win that lottery jackpot, we'll be able to buy every item on our wish list. We'll also quit our job and do what we really want to do. We carry the picture of our perfect life intact in our minds from year to year. The particulars in our dream vision may change over time as our tastes and priorities shift, but what remains constant in our consciousness is the feeling of satisfaction we will enjoy once our ship comes in and we have it made.

I don't want to smash your dreams, but the truth of the matter is that *no one has it made.* No matter how much money, or power, or fame you may have, you are still prone to all the pitfalls and mishaps of this world. Kings and billionaires get out of bed and stub their toes. The most gorgeous starlets and models feel the ache of loneliness and unrequited love. The most powerful politicians and business executives still encounter numerous frustrations and disappointments. Nobody, regardless of his or her wealth, position, or popularity, has a perfect ride through this life. Some people may have more and do more than others, but that doesn't mean that they are more happy or fulfilled. Even wise men have suffered reversals, lost touch with their wisdom, and experienced periods of fear and misery. Read the biographies of famous and rich people: you will discover that most of them, in spite of the privilege of their position and grandeur of their surroundings, lived lives filled with doubt, bitter conflicts, and emotional turmoil. Albert Einstein, revered as one of the greatest minds of the twentieth century, said that if he had had his life to live over again, he would have preferred to be a shoemaker.

When we think of someone as having it made, it is always from our perspective, which is outside that other person's actual experience. We see the surface of his situation—the expensive possessions, people applauding—and imagine how these external trappings would make us feel if they were transferred into our set of personal circumstances. If, instead, we were able to step inside his circumstances and experience his inner feelings, we might feel that he was more afflicted than fortunate.

Go back and look at the image that you have of your dream life, the state of affairs in which you've got it made. It's a static picture; everything that really matters in your life has happened already. Indeed, regard the phrase, "got it made." The key word, *made,* is in the past tense.

What lies behind our concept of having it made is our rational practice of taking an idea and projecting it in a straight, unwavering line into the future. In this instance, we envision a moment of total contentment, and then we mentally extend that moment to encompass the remainder of our earthly life. In this way we are trying to abolish change, eschewing anything that is new.

However, this whole world is constantly in flux; it is ever transforming and changing. We are perfectly capable of adapting, minute by minute, to all kinds of varying conditions and shifting situations. Indeed, we enjoy coping with the unexpected. That's what games are all about. It's our rational minds that have such a devotion to static pictures. Even though the mind operates at lightning speed and can flit from topic to topic, it is most comfortable following well-worn patterns. Therefore, it regards that which is stable and dependable as ideal. Look again at how repetitious most of your thoughts are each day. While our spirits welcome adventure and our bodies are routinely making millions of adjustments each second, our minds prefer to dwell on topics they already know. To the mind, the most appealing feature of "having it made" is that there will no longer be anything unexpected, challenging, or threatening to cope with. In other words, nothing to provoke it into extending itself into new and unknown territory. However, without the stimulation of new and sometimes uncomfortable things, the mind itself will become bored and discontent.

Recall a time when there was a special item that you desired more than anything, and you got it. It may have been a car, an item of clothing, an object of art, or an electronic device. Do you still have it? How do you feel about it now? Once the sparkling new quality has worn off, has your attitude toward it changed? Does it have certain drawbacks or imperfections that mar your sense of satisfaction? Clothing, cars, and electronic devices ultimately wear out, break down, and become obsolete. Even works of art can become damaged, or so much a part of our everyday scene that we fail to notice them. Slowly or rapidly, everything in this dimension is changing and transforming, and this dynamic process encompasses our own interests, fascinations, and desires.

When I was a teenager I worked on a golf course. My boss, the greenkeeper, was one of the most astute turf managers in the region. He had learned the trade from his father, who had been both a golf pro and a greenkeeper. Keeping a golf course in superb condition involves a constant battle with the weather, insects and disease, dilapidated equipment, complaining golfers, and employees who are often ill paid and transient. There is always a considerable gap between the actual state of a golf course and the ideal of an unblemished carpet of healthy grass that each greenkeeper strives for.

My boss was highly regarded by his peers, and many of them frequently came to him for advice. The common theme among these men was that, if they only had a bigger budget, a few more pieces of equipment, and maybe some favorable weather, they would be able to maintain a perfect golf course. My boss had a different attitude. He liked to quote an old-time greenkeeper who said: "You could give me twice the number of men, twice the budget, and a barn full of new equipment—and none of it would prevent some gopher from digging a hole on the first green at six o'clock on a Sunday morning."

Life is a fluid situation. Not only are we capable of coping with the unanticipated, there is even a supreme thrill in doing so. Consider that perfection, instead of being an unchanging, stable state, is a process of ongoing culmination. This moment is perfect, because everything is right where it needs to be at this time. In the next moment, the position of everything will have changed, and these new positions will be the appropriate and perfect ones for that moment.

When it comes to having it made, realize this: every moment is new. Every minute offers you a fresh start, a blank slate. You can be at the pinnacle of the world one moment, then slip and fall flat on your face in the next. Conversely, you could be at rock bottom, unemployed and broke—and have a song in your heart. The set of circumstances that surrounds us at any given moment is neutral. It is up to us to determine how we feel, content or dissatisfied, hopeful or hopeless, at every step along the way. Society looks at external conditions, which is all it is capable of doing, and makes general, stereotyped assumptions about what these conditions mean. However, all meaning comes from within ourselves, not from outward appearances. Life is action, and action involves fluctuations between expansion and contraction, advances and retreats, exertion and rest.

The key factor that will determine how you will encounter the inevitable ups and downs of each day is your own attitude. If you take it as a personal affront each time something doesn't work out exactly as you had wished, you're in for a lot of frustration and misery; your vision of the perfect life will forever be in the mythical future, unchanging and unattainable. In contrast, if you go through your day with an attitude of acceptance and amusement, you will be able to revel in the elegant beauty of the way events unfold and fit together, even when they are not following your plans and desires. And then you may discover yourself in a moment of true satisfaction and contentment—a moment in which you will *have it made.* The more you can immerse yourself in an awareness of the ongoing, transforming perfection all around you, the more of these contented moments you will enjoy. You can have it made at any time, even when you are in the dentist's chair getting a root canal. The secret lies in accepting the dynamic nature of this world and knowing that every moment is a fresh opportunity to smile, cooperate, and become fully involved in the marvel of living in physical reality.

Chapter Ten

Vibrations

Almost everyone has seen Einstein's famous Theory of Relativity, in which $E = mc^2$. This theory holds that energy and matter are interchangeable. What we think of as physical matter is highly condensed and concentrated energy; energy made solid, you might say.

Both energy and matter have a common characteristic: vibration. All atoms, molecules, and aggregations of these small particles vibrate. Energy itself is identified and classified by the frequency of its vibration. Certain energy vibrations are those that we see as visible light. Others we hear, as sound. Still others we feel, as heat or even as electric shock. All of these seemingly different forms of energy can be arranged along a numerical scale, according to frequency. We experience the slower frequencies as sound, the intermediate ones as light, and the higher frequencies as microwaves, x-rays, and nuclear radiation. This band of frequencies, known as the electromagnetic spectrum, may extend infinitely into lower and higher frequencies that we have no way of measuring, much less comprehending.

It is worth keeping in mind that everything we see, hear, and taste can be described as corresponding to a specific frequency on this electromagnetic scale. Even our brain activity and emotional feelings produce vibrational frequencies that are highly characteristic for each emotion or type of thought. Indeed, every emanation you produce—every sound you make, every odor you emit, every idea you think, every emotion you feel, every one-of-a-kind protein your body makes—everything has a distinct, quantifiable vibration.

Since we are spirits within a body, we also exist on spiritual frequencies. While these spiritual vibrations cannot be measured with our current technology, they can be inwardly felt. Beyond the mental brainwaves that can be traced out on graph paper from an electroencephalograph machine, there is a more subtle quality of *awareness,* which is beyond the present capacity of science to ascertain. It is, however, a persistent, inherent quality of who we are.

There are many documented cases where a person's heart has stopped, brain activity has ceased, and, by standard definitions, they are dead and inert. Then they revive, literally come back to life. Their accounts of their experiences, from the instant when physical life ceased until it started up again, indicate motion, feeling, and thought, all measurable vibrations in this world. Yet the machines to which they were hooked up didn't record a thing. Wherever they were, the vibrations they were experiencing and producing were real enough for the person to remember them vividly. But they were too subtle for the machines. They were beyond the electromagnetic spectrum on which this world exists.

For now we will confine ourselves to the electromagnetic frequencies that encompass the parameters of our earthly life. It is a pretty vast place, even if it may only be a tiny segment of the larger reality. There are billions of distinct vibrations. A number of these frequencies carry varying shades of the color red. Another frequency, or set of frequencies, manifest to us as the musical note B flat. And still another narrow band of frequencies will serve as a channel for sending a stream of information through thin air, perhaps financial data, or the programs of our favorite radio station.

In our normal waking life, we receive and send out multitudes of frequencies every second. The frequencies of light and sound and heat are the most apparent ones to us. We see and hear thousands of frequencies all at once, and we project a continuous multitude of frequencies. Our measurable brainwave patterns range from zero to twenty-eight cycles per second; when we are engaged in normal conscious thought and activity, our mental vibrations bounce up and down this range.

Our emotional states also correspond to certain frequencies. Some years ago scientists actually pinpointed a vibration that they termed the *giggle frequency*. At one or more times, every one of us has had the experience of being with friends, joking around, and engaging in light-hearted repartee. The collective mood of this gathering rises to the point where everyone is laughing with abandon, and any word or gesture will only provoke further bursts of uncontrollable laughter. At such moments, everyone present is vibrating at the giggle frequency, and mirth is unavoidable.

At another point on the scale, the vibration of anger is so powerful that it can be perceived, almost as an independent physical presence. Imagine a crowded restaurant. Two patrons at adjoining tables become embroiled in a violent argument. Voices are raised, curses are uttered, plates of food are hurled, and chairs are knocked over. The combatants are escorted out of the room, yet the residue of their anger hangs like a thick, acrid odor over the entire room. All conversation and laughter has ceased, and the lingering vibration of animosity depresses the frequency of everyone for some time, intimidating them from speaking boldly or joking. At one time or another we have all felt this palpable sensation of anger and observed the dampening effect it will have on everyone's mood for long moments after the actual outburst.

Consider that each emotional state we experience exists as an independent, identifiable frequency. When our personal vibrations match that frequency, we feel that emotion. At the center of our being, we are calm, still, and neutral. Yet, just as our thinking process can be hijacked by soap opera chatter and gossip if we don't consciously choose our thoughts, so too we can be influenced, even manipulated, into feel-ing certain emotions when we are exposed to certain well-crafted cues. It's like driving through the countryside and feeling sad and depressed when we encounter patches of fog and rain, and then becoming happy and cheerful when the clouds part and the sun illuminates our way. If we don't consciously decide how we wish to feel about and react to events in our daily lives, external influences will direct us to produce certain emotional responses, whether these responses are to our benefit or not.

As an illustration of how completely we can relinquish control of our emotions to outside influences, consider the movies. Composers have long known that certain musical notes, tempos, and tones can elicit very specific responses in most people who hear them. The background music in a movie is specifically designed to set the emotional tone of each scene: mournful violins for sadness or tragedy, bouncy melodies and rhythms for comedy, and tense, strained notes for suspense or horror. If you want to see just how effective the musical vibrations are in molding your emotional responses, watch a horror movie with the sound turned off. The film will lose most of its scary impact, and many of the scenes will seem stupid or downright funny.

Certain colors and visual images can also lead us toward a desired response. A picture of kittens and flowers in a sunny field can inspire feelings of relaxation and acceptance, while a stark, black-and-white photograph of a polluted industrial site is more likely to elicit feelings of revulsion and disgust. Also, visual representations of situations we have experienced and emotions we have felt can stimulate our memories to the point where we relive the feeling of that experience. For example, the picture of a man or woman in formal attire who has unknowingly lost the seat of his pants or the back of her gown may stir up the mem-ory of an occasion when we were similarly embarrassed. All of these examples illustrate how commonplace and easy it is for us to have our emotional frequencies set or changed by external stimuli.

Of course, influencing and manipulating our emotional responses is the business of advertisers and the news media. Advertisers use certain sounds and images to annoy us and thus to get our attention, as well as comforting music and attractive scenes to seduce us into buying their products. News broadcasts often begin with stirring musical introductions, usually featuring horns and drums to set the emotional tone that they have something authoritative and important to say to us. Closer to home, family members, co-workers, and friends are constantly projecting their emotional vibrations at us and sending us cues about which types of vibrations they want from us in return.

In the same way that we have the power to choose each one of our thoughts, and to stop thinking about a particular topic at any time, we have the power to determine with which emotional frequency we will resonate. External stimuli will always be pouring in, and the unaware will allow themselves to be swayed one way and another by the ideas and moods that are projected at them. Become aware that the power always resides within you to decide what you will think and how you will feel about it.

Picture a vast array of shelves. The shelves that are at and slightly above eye level are labeled: patience, cooperation, relaxation, and serenity. As you look upward you see that other shelves are marked fulfillment, happiness, joy, and exhilaration. You cast your eyes downward and notice that some of these shelves are designated: jealousy, sadness, fear, anger, and hatred. You are always vibrating, always projecting frequencies that will correspond with one or another of these emotional slots. While you can be influenced by external events and moods, the fundamental and ultimate power to determine your frequency resides within you.

In effect, you can dial a vibration in the same way that you can select a frequency on the radio to hear a desired form of music. If you want to be happy, elevate your vibration until it is in tune with the frequency of happiness. As a vibration which is independent of all individuals, that frequency is *always there*. You can ride along on it in an upbeat mood whenever you desire. At other times you may want to be reverent and reflective, and you can adjust your frequency so that it aligns with those temperaments.

One of the underlying conditions of this physical world is the phenomenon of entrainment, by which a strong vibration will induce weaker vibrations to align with its frequency. This phenomenon can be observed in a room with several pendulum clocks. Within a short time, all of the pendulums will swing back and forth in unison. Likewise, the heartbeat of an infant who is being held by its mother will synchronize with the mother's pulse. If you walk into a room where twenty people are laughing and smiling, you will begin to smile, without even knowing what is so funny. You can employ this property of entrainment to change your emotional vibration. If you are tense and stressed, listen to soothing music. If you are unhappy, and truly want to elevate your mood, look in the mirror, smile, and start to laugh. It doesn't matter if the laughter is forced. If you smile into a mirror and laugh for three or four breaths, the vibration of that laughter through your body will raise your emotional frequency to a level of optimism and well being.

Just as we hear sounds and see light over a wide range of frequencies, we have also come into this life to explore and get to know the whole spectrum of human emotions. So there will be times when the appropriate reaction to events around us will be frustration, sadness, indignation, or anger. What is important to keep in mind is that you can visit each one of these frequency levels, learn what they represent, where they can fit into your overall development, and where they will function only as obstacles to your further refinement. Just like going to a zoo or a museum, you can visit each one of these emotions without locking yourself in the exhibit and remaining there for years. Remind yourself, frequently, that the center of your being is eternally unperturbed and neutral.

Frequently, a person will unconsciously allow himself to habitually inhabit a particular emotion, as if he was born with it, like an invisible yet permanent appendage. Perhaps he was once betrayed or cheated; as a result he decides that he will never trust anyone again. He holds onto this vibration of suspicion and carries it into each one of his subsequent relationships. In doing so, he sabotages any potentially rewarding relationships with people who are trustworthy, because the vibration of suspicion will not allow him to connect and form bonds with anyone.

All the vibrations we project are dynamic: that is, they are in constant motion. They are forever seeking other vibrations with which they are compatible. In the above example, a person who projects a vibration of suspicion will be consistently attracted to people who are devious and deceptive. As the old saying goes, you get what you give.

Also, although we have the power to determine which types of vibrations we will produce, the dynamic character of this energy prevents us from keeping it to ourselves. We may like to think that we can indulge in all kinds of spiteful and unpleasant feelings in secret, but the fact is that our every emotion flows outward from ourselves, just as light pours forth from the sun. Most people won't pick up on our secret passions and resentments, because they are preoccupied with their own concerns. Nonetheless, each one of our hiddenmost feelings can be perceived by others. We've all had the experience of putting on a brave face when something is inwardly troubling us, only to have a close friend or relative confront us and say, "Something's wrong; what's troubling you?"

We are creator beings. Not only do we bring physical objects, like bridges and machines, into manifestation on this earth, we also create vibrations. Once we have sent them forth, these vibrations will persist way beyond our earthly lives. All the emotional energy we have emitted is still bouncing around the universe. We can recall, through the faculty of memory, our own vibrations of former experiences and relive the impact they had on us years earlier. And we have developed technologies that allow us to record and replay the emotions that were expressed by people many years ago. Consider that you can watch a movie that was made sixty years ago, one in which all the actors who appeared in it have died. As you watch the movie, those actors come back to life. Their performances are as fresh as the day they were filmed, and the emotions they project have lost none of their immediacy or relevance. When you watch a film like *Casablanca,* haven't you felt your own emotions aligning with those expressed by Humphrey Bogart and Ingrid Bergman?

In an earlier chapter, I mentioned that we deposit a sort of psychic dust wherever we go. This "dust" is actually the enduring vibration of our emotions and thoughts. Certain individuals possess high sense perception, and one aspect of this enhanced sensitivity is an ability to tune in to the lingering vibration of past events. These people are sometimes employed by police departments to help locate missing persons and decipher clues at crime scenes. Whether we are gifted with high sense perception or not, we all possess an ability to tune into vibrations from another time or another place. As a way of confirming this fact to yourself, look at photographs of people's faces. The most apparent thing you will notice right away is the emotion the person was emanating when the photograph was taken. The energetic vibration of whatever emotion the person was feeling literally flows out from the photograph.

If you study photographs of people's faces in a detached way, you will begin to perceive the underlying characteristics of their personality as well, because kindness, deceit, diligence, and arrogance all have distinct vibrational fingerprints.

What would a photograph of you reveal to others? Bear in mind that your friends, co-workers, and strangers don't have to laboriously study your picture to figure out who you are, because you are continuously announcing and revealing yourself to the world every minute, by the vibrations you project.

We possess many vibrational attributes. Some of them, like our thoughts and emotions, can change rapidly and dramatically. At the same time, we each display a more persistent vibrational structure by which we can be identified as a distinct individual in this world. By way of analogy, think of snowflakes.

A single snowstorm produces an uncountable number of snowflakes, no two of which are exactly alike. Although all snowflakes are hexagonal—six sided—the potential for variation within that single form is so great that each flake has an arrangement of ice crystals that is distinctly different from every other snowflake. Billions and billions of snowstorms have occurred throughout Earth's history, and every tiny snowflake they have produced has been a new, never-before-seen creation.

Each one of us is unique in many ways. We exhibit specific vibrational signatures that belong to us alone, just like the peculiar shape of each individual snowflake.

Let's look at one small slice of the electromagnetic spectrum, that section of frequencies that we interpret as sound. If I play the note C on the piano and on the flute, they will sound alike, and yet you will easily be able to distinguish which sound came from the piano, and which from the flute. In addition to the fundamental note that is played, numerous harmonics of the note are also produced. The strength and softness of this array of harmonics varies markedly from one instrument to another, and it is the particular combination of overtones that gives each instrument its distinctive sound.

This quality also applies to the human voice. We all produce a different combination of overtones when we speak, and thus each voice has a unique sound signature. Science and technology have devised instruments that produce voice prints, which are used to ascertain the positive identity of a person, much the same as a fingerprint.

The vibration of our voice grows out of the more subtle, multi-layered emanations of our personality. Our personality is similar to our body, in that it is a unique set of traits we inhabit and display for the duration of this one lifetime. Even more than our body, we identify with this personality, yet it is also an acquired form that our soul uses to explore and experience this dimension of reality. While we are all connected in the unity of All, each soul is also an individual entity with access to infinite creativity. We employ this limitless creative potential to manifest bodies and personalities that possess a wide range of one-of-a-kind properties.

A sampling of some of the traits by which we can be singled out from every other member of the human race includes: the sound of our voice, the pattern of our fingerprints, the arrangement of pigments in our eyes, the chemical structure of our proteins, and our specific body odor (ask any bloodhound).

As such, this amalgamation of highly individual properties and traits is the identity that we have chosen to have in this lifetime. Moment to moment, we can decide which thoughts and emotions we wish to have. Yet, there is a whole set of background vibrations that are going to be with us from our first breath to our last. These vibrations will take form as the color of our eyes, shape of our skeleton, shade of our skin, sensitivity to allergens, and numerous other physical characteristics. Under the surface, there are also personality traits, expressed as preferences, aversions, obsessions, and attitudes that serve as a resonating psychological framework within which we will pursue most of our life's activities.

We can modify and even significantly alter portions of our personality framework, and for some of us that is one of the tasks we came into this life to perform. Again, remember that this whole setup is dynamic, so that changes, minor and significant, will always be occurring. Still, in general, our personality will serve as a kind of standard vibration by which most people will recognize and know us during this lifetime.

Sometimes, our vibrations will thoroughly synchronize with those of another person. Just as each of us possesses and exhibits numerous unique vibrations, so too our individual emanations will match up harmoniously or disharmoniously with the emanations of other persons and things. Have you ever shared a knowing look with someone, even a total stranger? In that moment, you and the other person were of one accord; you were on the same wavelength. When we achieve these pinnacles of full cooperation, understanding, and acceptance, we have completely aligned our vibratory frequency with another person's. These moments of *communion* are usually fleeting instants, yet they give us a glimpse of the true state of unity that exists among us all at the deep, still, soul-to-soul-level.

In music, two or more notes that harmonize with each other are described as being in *concord*. Notes that are not harmonious are referred to as *discord*. In more general usage, we use the word concord to describe an agreement, treaty, or pact between individuals, groups, even nations. Discord can lead to alienation, arguments, and fights. If a vibration of discord is maintained long enough and amplified sufficiently, it can produce riots, insurrections, and war.

As we thread our way through this world, each one of us seeks other persons, activities, and objects that resonate harmoniously with ourselves. We will instinctively shun or avoid whatever we sense as discordant. Yet, due to the dualistic tendency of our thinking process, and the fact that we can rapidly change our mental opinions and emotional moods, disharmonies will frequently arise. However, this process works both ways. We can set up oppositions that lead to discord and conflict, and we are equally capable of transforming discord into resolution and incorporating diverse elements into a coherent, pleasing whole. We can arrange splashes of paint in a way that the colors clash and hurt our eyes, or we can use the same colors to create the most lovely designs and pictures.

I mentioned earlier that vibrations tend to seek out other frequencies with which they are compatible, or harmonious. As vibrating beings, we will find some people attractive, some repellent, and others neutral. Has it ever struck you as odd that, while you may have a wide circle of friends, you don't know the neighbors who live just five doors away from you? There are no laws or physical barriers to prevent you from meeting. Yet your paths have never crossed, not at a public forum, in a store, or at someone's party. There are other people in your immediate proximity whom you encounter from time to time, but you have never connected or related to them in any significant way. You are only aware of them in the way a passenger on a bus sees pedestrians through the window as the bus is rolling by.

Here is another old saying: birds of a feather flock together. In the realm of vibration, compatible frequencies will engage with one another and mesh together. Just think of the way musical notes combine harmoniously in a major chord. Conversely, incompatible vibrations will not join or mesh together. In effect, they will bounce off or be invisible to one another.

As an example of how distinct some vibrational levels can be from others, consider a seedy, crime-ridden neighborhood. Drug dealers rule the streets, apartments are regularly burglarized, gun battles erupt on the sidewalks; the weak are terrorized, robbed, and bullied. Except for Mrs. Harper. She's ninety-two years old and has lived in the same apartment for the past sixty-five years. It was a lovely neighborhood when she first moved in. Over the decades, as the area declined and her friends and neighbors died or moved away, she remained in her tidy, first-floor apartment. Every morning she sweeps off her front stoop, and the sidewalk out to the curb. She devoutly attends Mass each day at a church three blocks away, and on Sundays she gives the pastor a fresh-baked loaf of raisin pumpernickel bread. Year in and year out, she goes about her business unmolested. Her apartment has never been burglarized, and she has never been robbed or threatened, despite all the mayhem occurring around her each day. To all the thieves and ruffians of the neighborhood, she is invisible. What is her secret? Her plane of vibration is so different from everyone else's that she is like the air itself; she attracts no notice.

You may think Mrs. Harper is just a fanciful figmentof my imagination, with no flesh and blood counterpart in the real world. But there are millions of people around the world today, living in war zones and other highly dangerous environments, who go on about their business each day and live relatively, even completely unscathed lives. They do so because they do not inhabit the planes of fear, anger, violence, and retribution that are prevalent all around them.

To illustrate with a less extreme example, consider your own circumstances. You have a number of acquaintances, and a smaller circle of friends with whom you usually socialize. You are aware of other groupings of friends, and perhaps you wish to belong to one of those other groups. What is it that sets them apart from you? Wealth may be a factor, but it is not the sole determinant. Several people in the group you aspire to join make considerably less money than you do. The members of this group belong to different professions and faiths, even to different political parties. Yet there is a common thread that ties them together; throughout the years they seek out and enjoy each other's company. This group is not fixed or exclusive. Some members move out of town, and new people are welcomed in.

Such social groupings naturally form in each community, as people on similar vibratory planes congregate together. Think of these vibratory planes as domains of natural affinity. Whatever plane you are on, you attract and are attracted to others who are on that same plane. If you are not particularly happy with your group of associates at present, you must change your own vibration to fit in with a group that you see as more desirable.

Consider that these various vibratory levels correspond to levels of density. We are all here in physical reality, and the material world is a dense dimension, perhaps the most dense of them all. In this dimension, everything is so dense that it appears as solid matter. However, on this plane of existence, there are greater and lesser degrees of density. We readily observe this in the world around us. Solid objects are more dense than liquids, which are more dense than air. Even within these divisions, there are differences in density. Lead is more dense than granite, which is more dense than wood, which is more dense than paper. Among the liquids, honey is more dense than water, and water is more dense than alcohol.

In a similar way, we can regard our own vibrations as being more or less dense. People who are weighed down by cares and negative attitudes can be seen as inhabiting a denser vibratory level than happier people. How do we describe a person who is brimming with the joy of life? We say that he or she is *lighthearted.* And so they are. Although still on the material plane, they have risen into the least dense layers of it. Similarly, we describe an individual who is overwhelmed with concern or sadness as having a *heavy heart.*

Imagine that density corresponds to awareness. The more unaware we are, the more dense our consciousness is. As we learn and incorporate our increased awareness into our habitual thoughts and actions, our vibratory rate rises. As we continue to learn and refine ourselves in this material dimension, we rise to higher and higher levels, until it is apparent to others on this physical plane that we have progressed to such a state that they describe us as being *enlightened.* This one word expresses two qualities: radiance and lack of density. This term is used when speaking about saints, philosophers, gifted scientists, and artists.

What about you? Do you feel that to exhibit this radiance you must belong to a select group that has been determined at birth? That only the lucky and accomplished can ever attain enlightenment? On the contrary, this state is accessible to all. Remember that you are an eternal and divine being, and that outside of this physical plane you already are an enlightened and exalted soul. Look a little deeper into your reasons for being in this dimension. Before you were born, you consciously and willingly accepted the cloak of physical density, to further experience all the dimensions of reality, and to develop new aspects and facets of your infinite soul. The process of this journey of discovery involves the experience of the densest emotions and the harshest and heaviest physical conditions. However, it is also part of the process for you to ascend from the densest to the lightest levels of this dimension.

Each day we will be confronted with numerous situations to which we can respond in either an uplifting or a negative manner. In the same way that we have the power to choose each one of our thoughts, we also have the power to choose our emotional responses. If we are consciously determined to inhabit the higher frequencies and ascend into the levels of less density, we will become consistent in responding with kindness and goodwill. These vibrations will have a real effect in the world. By revealing and projecting our own inner radiance, we can elevate the frequency of the whole material plane.

Chapter Eleven

Plenty of Everything
for Everybody

You are a creator being. Outside of this physical dimension, you have vastly greater powers than you can even remember when you are here on Earth. You have willingly come here to work on an exceedingly minute, material level. However, your connection to your larger, powerfully creative self has not been severed. It may be obscured by the fog of forgetfulness you passed through as you entered the physical plane, but it is still intact. Your imagination is the pipeline through which you can open up the channel to your creativity.

This world is a workshop to which we come to employ and further develop our creative potentialities. Look around whatever room or setting you happen to be in. Every manmade object—the building, the furniture, all decorations and electrical devices—existed first as a vision in someone's mind before it was brought into physical manifestation. That is the power we have. First we imagine, and then we bring the imagined object into full material expression. Like magicians, we have conjured the entire built world out of thin air.

Each day we use, live in, and pass by innumerable examples of the objects we have manifested. Yet we still labor under a gigantic delusion. This fallacy is drummed into us every day by politicians, economists, relatives, and friends. In spite of overwhelming evidence to the contrary, the prevailing belief in society is that we live in a world of scarcity.

The story goes something like this: We live in a physical, finite world. Everything has its limits. If you have a hundred dollars and you go out and spend it, you will have no more money. If you have a quart of milk and you drink it, it will be all gone. There is only so much food, air, water, toilet paper, cashmere sweaters, etc. The main error with this idea is that it views the world as a static place. According to this idea, the only change that occurs is that the quantities of things keep declining. Again, all the evidence points to the opposite conclusion. What the originators of the scarcity theory seemed to miss entirely is that, within the physical boundaries of this world, things are constantly rearranging themselves and transforming from one thing into another. Take food as an example. We may have only one hundred bushels of wheat on hand today. But we can plant that wheat and harvest over fifty times as much. The productive capability of this world is limitless. Where life is concerned, physical space seems to be the only real limitation. In arable areas, the land is literally carpeted with life. Plants cover every square inch of the ground. In fact, growing at different heights, as grasses, shrubs, and trees, they actually cover each piece of ground several times. The soil teems, not only with the roots of plants and myriad burrowing animals, insects, and worms, but also with an uncountable number of microorganisms. Numerous animals and birds intermix with the plants above the ground, along with insects and many, many more microorganisms.

The seas are also brimming with life, all the way down to the cold and highly pressurized depths of thirty thousand feet. Even the harshest environments on Earth, from the frozen arctic regions to the hot and waterless desert areas, are home to a remarkable number of hardy creatures. We have even found tiny forms of life wafting around in the higher levels of the atmosphere, and in rocks and oil deposits thousands of feet underground. Our human imaginations must strain to enumerate and comprehend the extent and variety of all the life that occupies this planet, the enormous scope of which suggests the design and input of one or several very highly developed imaginative beings. Although some species may be extinct, or nearly extinct, new forms keep coming into being. The whole order of mammals, to which we belong, appeared on Earth only a little over one hundred million years ago, at a time when dinosaurs were dominant. Today, the dinosaurs have disappeared, while the wide variety of mammals inhabits every geographical region of the Earth.

Even today, new species are coming into being. While the time frame for larger organisms to develop may involve thousands or millions of years, bacteria and viruses can change and mutate so quickly that there are strains and types of bugs around today that our grandparents never knew. Indeed, we seem to be inadvertently working with the bacteria and viruses to bring new members of their families into being. Our widespread use of antibiotics and other toxins only incites them to branch out into new species more rapidly.

This Earth is not a place of scarcity, but one of creative abundance. This principle applies equally to the realm of human activity. Our creative capacity is unbounded. So the point to keep in mind is: **This is a big world. There is plenty of everything for everybody.** Remember, we are creator beings. We can turn ideas into material objects. This world is adaptable and transformable, so that whatever we decide we need or want can be brought into physical manifestation. Whatever you want, if you want it without conflict or reservation, you can have. With respect to physical things, the world is full of stuff. If you want a refrigerator, a gold bracelet, or a hot fudge sundae, they are all readily available. In the more intangible areas of our lives, where our needs and desires are usually more strongly felt but often not as well articulated, this principle also applies. If you want power, you can acquire it. Respect, recognition—and the big one, love—can be yours, if this is what you truly want. In the same manner, if you go looking for trouble, you will find that, too.

When I was in college, I worked nights as a security guard. One of my jobs was at an industrial site. One guard worked from 4 pm to midnight, and then I worked from midnight to 8 am. Each shift we would make hourly tours of the building, and fill out a report form. The guard on the four to twelve shift was a quiet living, semi-retired fellow who wasn't looking for any excitement. For me, the job provided a quiet place to study in between watch tours, as well as money for school expenses.

The neighborhood was almost deserted after business hours, and our reports, week after week, described an unchanging routine. Except for the three or four times when the regular evening guard took a day off. On each occasion, the same young man filled in for him. Ambitious and over-eager, this guy yearned to be an action hero. He was looking for trouble. And he kept finding it. Every night that I relieved this fellow, his report was filled with accounts of threatening incidents and attempted break-ins. One night he even managed to inject himself into an argument between two men across the street! Trouble swarmed around him like flies on a ripe garbage can. The regular guard and I weren't looking for trouble, and we never attracted any.

In a previous chapter, I mentioned that the vibrations we produce seek out similar, compatible vibrations, and are essentially invisible to frequencies that have incompatible qualities. A well-known phrase from the Bible says, "seek and you shall find." *You will find whatever you choose to look for.*

What are you currently looking for, consciously or unconsciously? If you want to know, look at the current circumstances of your life, and you will see what you have already found. If you are not happy with certain situations or aspects of your life, you need to change what you're looking for.

It's good to begin by examining the root motivations and desires that led you to seek out what you have presently attracted. Be honest and also gentle with yourself. Many times we will seek out an unfulfilling or unrewarding position or relationship because we feel that we are inherently unworthy and want justification for feeling sorry for our mediocre, miserable selves. Self-loathing, feeling we are not good enough, is a prevalent human condition. To step out of this cozy quagmire of self-pity, remember your divine nature. You are a manifestation of Almighty Perfection, forever. Whatever wonderful things appeal to your tastes, you deserve them. Similarly, realize that if you engage in dangerous activities because you are seeking the thrill of flirting with disaster, you may survive with some spellbinding tales to tell, or your physical life may be extinguished like a candle flame in a hurricane.

Actualization is a neutral process. It doesn't distinguish between positive and negative. Keep in mind that you are the one at the controls; with your desire and imagination you are the one who is attracting goods and qualities into your life. As the saying goes, you reap what you sow; therefore, pay close attention to the seeds you are selecting for the garden that is your life.

At this point you may be skeptical, for there are things that you have wanted, consistently and fervently, for many years, and yet not attained them. In these instances, we are usually waiting for another person, society, or the world at large to make the first move. We're perfectly willing to respond with respect, generosity, and affection if that is the way we are treated. To get this process of manifestation to work, there's one simple, yet effective trick: we must reverse the sequence of action. In other words, we must first become the quality we want to experience. If we want respect, we must first become respectful, of ourselves and others. If we yearn for love, we must be loving. When we create a quality within ourselves and then emanate it to the world at large, the world will respond by replicating that quality and sending it back to us. All we have to do is summon up the courage to take the first step.

Each one of us, through our actions and emotions, has the power to propagate and distribute kindness, compassion, and cooperation throughout the world. Or, we are just as capable of spreading distrust, envy, and hostility. The world is at our disposal to make of it what we will.

As a creative being, you are always manifesting things and situations in your life. If you are not pleased with your present surroundings or circumstances, look within, to your own beliefs and desires. In what way, even a perverse way, is your present life fulfilling your aims? Also, examine the mental picture you have constructed that tells you how the world works. This picture can be small and constrained, or it can be extensive, even open ended. This personal mental idea is what you project out into this physical world, and it sets boundaries and parameters within which you will move and think. These boundaries are not imposed by the laws of matter, but by what you believe to be possible, desirable, feasible, and attainable. If you feel penned in and restrained from doing what a deep inner prompting keeps insisting you came here to do, then unlock your shackles and roam freely.

This world is wildly productive. We manifest an abundance of wonderful material things every day. All the qualities of a happy and rewarding life are ours to manifest as well. Become generosity. Become joy. Become love.

Chapter Twelve

Pain

The bodies we inhabit have millions of nerve cells that alert us to changes in external conditions that might pose a threat to our health and physical well being. To compel us to respond with an appropriate protective action, the sensations we receive will elicit various forms of discomfort, irritation, or outright pain.

An instance of discomfort could be the chill that our body feels when the temperature drops, signaling that we had better put on additional clothes. Physical irritation, such as muscle stiffness or fatigue, serves to warn us to alter or cease certain motions to avoid overstraining ourselves. And outright pain, such as when we cut our finger on a piece of glass, lets us know that danger is upon us; it results in an immediate and abrupt change in our behavior so as to minimize or avoid any further injury.

We also experience a whole spectrum of pain whose origin is not physical. Although we may feel many variations of this pain—such as anguish, doubt, grief, depression, fear, and despair—these mental and emotional maladies will often cause and be accompanied by physical manifestations of pain as well, such as headaches, indigestion, and, over time, a whole catalog of degenerative diseases.

It is easy to view this physical dimension as predominantly a world of suffering and pain. Even on your best days, there are still painful interludes: you bruise your shin, or someone makes a particularly cutting or insulting remark about you. In all, pain is like ants at a picnic—uninvited, unwelcome, yet inevitable.

Most of us have certain pains—both physical and emotional—that are chronic, pains that we have come to believe are incurable. However, the spiritual realm from which we emerged into this world was a dimension without pain. And when we first entered into our body, that vehicle, in almost all instances, was perfect in shape and function, and pain free.

I'm sure that at least several times in your life, when you have been wracked with severe pain or emotional trauma, you have sent forth the question into the wide universe: Why me? What did I do to deserve this?

Let's return to one of the principles mentioned above. You chose to come into this world. You came here to learn. Your teachers are all around you, in all shapes, sizes, and demeanors. And perhaps the most powerful teacher this world has to offer is pain. Remember that everything in this world has a purpose. Pain serves many purposes, and they are all instructive. Each painful experience contains a lesson. To give a very simple example: If you step on a thorn, it tears your skin. You bleed, and it hurts. The pain of your torn and bleeding skin conveys the lesson to you that sharp, pointed objects are a threat to the function and health of the physical body. The world is full of thorns and other sharp, pointed objects, such as knives and various cutting tools, which have many constructive uses. By learning from our pain, we are able to employ these objects for our benefit, but at the same time refrain from using them in any inappropriate, self-destructive way. Of course, this is a very simple example, and it assumes that, from a single encounter with pain, we will learn what is necessary to avoid that pain in the future, and act accordingly.

Most of us have lived with one or more painful situations of long duration. Why does the pain persist? Would you believe that, for the most part, we are all very, very slow learners? You may think that I'm being flip, or making a cruel joke at your expense. But let me state the principle again: Pain has a purpose. It occurs to teach you a particular lesson. Once you have fully learned that lesson, accepted it, and incorporated the knowledge into the working pattern of your life—so that you are now thinking and acting differently than you did before—the pain will have served its purpose. Since this is a purposeful dimension, and a temporal one, all things that fulfill their purpose are then transformed. In the case of pain, once you have learned the lesson, it has no further purpose, and so it dissipates. It goes away; it vanishes.

Bear in mind that some of the things you have come here to learn are life lessons. It may take you decades, or even more than one lifetime, to fully learn them. An example of a life lesson may be self-assertion. You may chose a body that is rather small, and a physical constitution that is less than robust, to keep the issue of standing up for your rights at the forefront of all your interpersonal affairs. Or you may need to learn a lesson about greed. Throughout your life you will inherit and come into possession of many objects. But you will lack the financial resources to care for them properly, so that all these things you are avid to possess are constantly deteriorating and slipping away from you. Until you resolve this issue of compulsive possessiveness, you will suffer bitter pangs of loss every time an object escapes your sphere of ownership and control.

At this point I should emphasize that, just because we have ailments and lessons to learn does not mean we have done something wrong and are being punished for it. Throughout our infinite, eternal existence we are always experiencing and learning. Pain is not a punishment. It is simply a medium through which we develop more awareness and self-knowledge.

There's nothing that decrees this learning process has to take a long time; it's entirely up to the individual. We all have varying degrees of reluctance about accepting certain lessons, even though our stubbornness causes us to endure many years of pain.

In part, because of the amnesia we all take on when we enter this realm, we may have simply forgotten which issues and lessons we came here to encounter and resolve. However, there is an easy way to remember what those issues are. All we have to do is examine our lives and identify those factors that are causing us the most discomfort, agitation, and pain.

When you look at it this way, the process becomes more of an adventure. What is causing *you* pain? Do you suffer from a particular physical condition? Go back to when it first manifested, and look into the factors that played a part in its development. Some of your suffering may be due entirely to self-abusive physical habits, such as eating or drinking too much, and if so, the lesson may be that you need to learn to live in moderation.

This example may sound overly simple, but remember the dualistic feature of the rational mind, which leads to a tendency to split issues into their polar opposites and then to choose one side or the other. This dualistic temperament will frequently dispose a person to go to one polar extreme or the other. So we may eat too much or starve ourselves, promote permissive or repressive political and/or religious views, engage in relationships with manic naivete or morose cynicism. In all of these instances, we are taking a position that is at odds with the divine unity that is the true state of the universe. And whenever we are at odds with the truth, in one fashion or another, we will feel some form of pain.

Within the dualistic framework of our way of viewing the world, we are all here to learn how to strike a balance: actually, many balances, with respect to our physical practices, mental beliefs, and emotional responses. The widespread nature of certain physical and emotional complaints only confirms that these are lessons that every soul with a human nature has to learn.

Beyond the purely physical lessons of learning how to live properly within a human body, there are *millions* of other mental and emotional lessons for us to learn. Issues revolving around power, love, acceptance and rejection, safety and trust are a small sampling of the aspects of life we may be wrestling with.

Many times the manifestation of our pain is directly analogous to the situation we need to resolve. We may have a co-worker whose habits or statements constantly annoy us, and as we work alongside this person month after month we suffer from a persistent and sharp pain in the neck. At other times, as with dream images, the manifestation of our pain may be more symbolic in nature. A propensity to suffer from sore throats or laryngitis may indicate that we are too easily intimidated or reluctant to assert ourselves.

Many times, the most difficult persons and relationships in our lives are our greatest teachers. Consider that what bothers us the most about them is actually a reflection of our own not-so-pleasant qualities. Conflicts with other persons often indicate inner contradictions that we haven't resolved. Difficult relationships can be regarded as an invitation to look deep into our own character for aspects that could use some correction and improvement.

For any ailment that you have, ask yourself: What is the lesson? What is this condition here to teach me? When you are acutely troubled with terrible pain, you may even want to repeat the following phrase, almost like a mantra: Learn the lesson, lose the pain. Learn the lesson, lose the pain.

I experienced a very dramatic illustration of this principle one day. It was late afternoon, and I needed to go to the post office before it closed. As I was walking toward my car, I noticed a dead branch, suspended in a low hanging tree limb, right above the driveway. I jumped up to pull it out of the tree. However, the branch was more firmly entwined in the limb than I had thought, and when I grabbed its lower extremity, it did not move. Then the bottom portion of the branch abruptly snapped, and I, completely unbalanced, fell in a heap onto the driveway. I landed on my right hand, and the loose gravel dug deeply into my palm. My whole body was on fire with pain, and I could barely move my fingers. I was furious—with myself, the tree, the dead branch, the gravel in the road, and cruel life in general.

I remembered that I needed to get my mail, so I hobbled over to my car. It was a ten minute drive to the post office, and I had twelve minutes until closing time. My hand was throbbing with searing pain, and that pain was matched by my mental anguish and agitation. I was in the midst of a landscaping project, for which the use of my hand was absolutely essential. My deadline was three days away, and I couldn't afford any down time. Yet the nature of my injury was such that my hand would be useless for several days. I was fuming as I drove, cursing the tree and my own haplessness, when suddenly three words displaced my thoughts: *Learn the lesson.*

At once I stopped cursing and complaining, and sought out the lesson that this incident was meant to convey to me. I was powerfully motivated to uncover this teaching, because I was determined to complete my project on time. Due to my unreserved willingness to recognize what I needed to learn, the lesson instantly unfolded in my consciousness, before I was halfway to the post office. It had nothing to do with my project, dead branches, or loose gravel. These elements had only served as a lens to focus my attention on another more subtle, yet pressing matter. It was not a pretty issue, because it involved some of my firmly held opinions and attitudes. Under normal circumstances, I would have continued to sidestep and evade it. But now, the pain had placed the issue front and center in my consciousness.

Recognizing the lesson was the first step. To effect healing, I then had to accept this teaching and incorporate it into my life, which meant transforming my attitudes. I was confronted with a clear choice: hold onto my old attitudes, and live with the pain; or step out of my pettiness, let go of the cozy negative emotions I had harbored, and enter into a new level of relating and acting. If I chose not to change, my hand would hurt for a few days, then I would gradually recover its full use. There would be no permanent injury, but I would have postponed learning that lesson. However, I had already learned that, while you can postpone your lessons, you can't evade them altogether. They keep circling back into your life in various manifestations until you finally accept them and progress to the next level. In this case, I wanted to complete my project more than I wanted to hang onto some peevish attitudes. For the rest of the evening, I consciously and sincerely accepted the lesson and amended my prejudiced opinions. The next day, while slightly sore, my hand was fine, and fully able to work.

Beyond the fact that we can often be excruciatingly slow learners, there is another reason people suffer from so many chronic conditions and so much long-term mental anguish. It may sound ridiculous, but we will often cling to painful conditions and situations because we are afraid to face life without them. As uncomfortable or downright agonizing as it may be, our pain can also form a secure framework around our personal and working relationships. The handicap of our pain gives us a consistent excuse for avoiding certain activities and even shuts the door on our extending ourselves into new aspects of relating to other people. We are able to avoid chores that we have told ourselves we don't like, and, due to our infirmities, people will not push us into new and therefore threatening ways of doing things. We all like to feel safe, and all too frequently we use pain as an excuse for staying on the known and secure path of doing things as we have always done them. Even though a part of us yearns for the thrill of being fully present in the moment, of taking life as it comes, with all its unpredictable surprises and unanticipated wonders, another part of us craves security and stability, even if it involves discomfort and pain. For example, some people will remain in abusive relationships because they have a greater aversion to the uncertainties of establishing ties with new people.

Each one of us lives in a tiny bubble of what we personally know—persons, activities, geographical locations, ways of relating to others. This little bubble is but a small speck of the immense potential that is accessible to us in this world. We all have a greater or lesser degree of reluctance when it comes to encountering anything that is new, uncertain, and potentially dangerous or painful.

New things do, of course, enter our lives all the time. We encounter and seek out new products, new movies, and new acquaintances from time to time. What if you were to pop your little bubble altogether and step boldly into the vast, unknown world, with only your wits and your smile to protect and sustain you? Surely, you would survive. Remember, you are eternal.

Others have taken this leap, and the world is largely captivated by their exploits. We call them adventurers, pioneers, heroes. Each one of us carries that divine, daring spark. If we weren't a fearless risk taker, we would never have jumped into this physical world in the first place. Many times we become set in a pattern of acting and relating in the same habitual ways because we believe that any deviation from this path would expose us to unspeakable embarrassment and pain. We need to remind ourselves continually that we are indestructible, and that we came here for adventure and a wide variety of experiences. No lasting harm can come to us, for we will live on forever. If anything, by dropping what we have been clinging to, we may finally step out of the shadows of our pain and into the warm bright light of joyous living and fulfilling relationships. The whole world, full of wonders, beckons to us. All we have to do is step forward.

Oftentimes, our minds can sabotage our efforts to grow and heal. In the same way that the mind will resist our intention to temporarily stop thinking, it will also try to prevent us from setting aside well-worn patterns of painful memories and attitudes. Every time we experience emotional pain, it stems from a situation we already know. Even with respect to fear of future events, our fear and anxiety is based on our memories of previous experiences and responses in similar circumstances. When we incorporate a lesson that has been conveyed to us by pain, we change and alter our habitual ways of acting, perceiving, and responding emotionally. In all of these respects, we are stepping into unfamiliar and uncertain territory.

The rational faculty is one-dimensional, and it can deal comfortably only with what it already knows. The unknown, by definition, is *something that it cannot think about.* Hence, it recoils, throws up a wall of resistance and fear, and tells us it's better to endure the ills we already have, rather than exchanging them for something that could potentially be much, much worse. Ah, but what if it is better?

By cultivating a daily awareness of our eternal natures we will enter into a new relationship with pain, in which we will appreciate the instruction it offers us. We will understand that each lesson is an invitation to expand our consciousness and to enjoy deeper, more fulfilling relationships. Unfamiliar territories will become inviting, rather than frightening.

Here's something that perhaps no one has ever told you. Most healing can take place instantaneously. Whether it's a grave physical illness, or a mental or emotional disorder that has troubled you for years, you can be rid of it in an instant. There are many cases of spontaneous healings. They are usually termed miracles, for two reasons. First, instant recoveries completely baffle the medical authorities, and they can't claim the credit for any of their drug or surgical therapies. Second, society at large feels threatened by the prospect that each individual might possess such power, so the healing agency is described in mystical, mysterious terms, as something supernatural and outside of the individual. However, the power of instant healing is inside of you. Remember, you possess a divine nature. A portion of the All-mighty creative force that brought this entire universe into being resides within you. Always.

What does it require to effect a complete healing, instantaneous or otherwise? First, a decision. A firm, irrevocable decision to be well. Every person who has had a spontaneous healing has reached a point where, either consciously or subconsciously, they have faced up to a question: Do I truly want to be well? Incorporated in that question are these further questions: Am I ready to accept the lesson that this malady has been trying to teach me? By accepting the lesson, am I ready and willing to change my attitudes and behavior, to align with the teaching of this lesson? Finally, am I ready and willing to put aside all of the excuses, evasions, and expectations of special treatment that have accompanied this malady?

When a person can answer all of these questions with a resounding, unrestrained, and heartfelt YES! he or she is ready to heal. In cases of spontaneous healing, the decision is so strong and complete that the intention to be well immediately aligns and elevates the vibration of every cell in the body to a healthy state. Remember that dis-ease is an acquired condition. It is something that has piggybacked on top of a healthy body. The person was complete and whole before the condition came along; the illness is extra baggage. Each malady, pain, and dis-ease carries with it an important lesson to learn. The lesson itself is weightless, painless, and of great benefit. By cultivating the skill of ascertaining what the lesson is in each painful condition we experience, we can become adept at quickly extracting this lesson and incorporating it into our character. The pain or dis-ease, having thus accomplished its purpose, will fade away or transform.

In the case of a terminal illness, healing may not involve physical recovery. Rather, learning this climactic lesson fulfills the life purpose, and the person can enter into the next phase of their eternal life with no unfinished business in this world.

Keep in mind that you will never exhaust all the lessons that this world contains. In the case of life lessons, you may deal with a succession of variations on the theme of patience, or forgiveness, for your entire life. Also, as you master certain lessons, you will be presented with fresh opportunities to learn new things. So the potential always exists that, no matter how much you have already learned and improved, you can still be confronted with new challenges, and some of them can be quite arduous. However, if you maintain the attitude that there is a jewel of knowledge and refinement to be extracted from every experience, no matter how uncomfortable or even harrowing, and remember that you are an indestructible, eternal being, you'll be fine.

Chapter Thirteen

Positive and Negative Motivation

We are all faced with an ongoing series of choices and decisions to make. There is one very simple principle to use when choosing which path to pursue. Choose the option that you really want, even if it appears to be impractical, outlandish, or a ridiculous longshot. At first blush, such advice may appear to be so obvious that it isn't worth mentioning. However, quite frequently people will choose something that they do not really want. They will explain away their choice by saying that it was more feasible, more convenient, cheaper, more socially acceptable, etc. But they will rarely, if ever, be satisfied or happy with these choices. Usually, they will find themselves in a situation that is unpleasant, unfulfilling, or totally unbearable.

Has this ever happened to you? Have you ever asked yourself, why did I take this job? or, why did I ever agree to these terms? You have a lot of company. Almost everyone regrets making certain choices, and quite a few people, tragically, are stuck in unhappy situations for long periods of time. In most of these cases, their initial decision stemmed from a negative motivation.

Just what, exactly, are positive and negative motivations? A positive motivation is one where you are moving toward something that you want. A negative motivation is one where you are moving away from something that you don't want. It's astonishing how often we base our decisions on what we don't want, instead of what we want. This process is usually referred to as choosing the lesser of two evils. However, if you go to a restaurant and choose a meal that is unpalatable only because it is slightly less offensive than the other items on the menu, you are still going to wind up with indigestion and heartburn. The wise thing to do is leave that establishment and go to a place where the cooking agrees with your stomach. When you choose something only because it is not as bad as something else, you are still making a bad choice.

When we act from a negative motivation, we set up one thing as being totally unacceptable, and we are determined to avoid it at all costs. However, our mental focus is fixed upon what we do not want, while we are not as clear about exactly what it is that we want. Say, for example, you are looking for a job. In your last position you worked in a doctor's office, and you really did not like being in the presence of so many sick and ailing people. As you go through the job listings, you're not particularly drawn *to* any specific job; your main concern is not being involved again with sick people. So you automatically ignore and reject all listings that have anything to do with health. The most dominant idea in your mind is, I'll do *anything but* health care. So you take a job in an insurance company. As far as you're concerned, it could be a restaurant, a factory, a school—anything but the health field. After only a few days, you hate your new job. Your supervisor is a tyrant, and the work does not interest you. However, what is worst of all is that your co-workers are chronically ill and complaining. They take numerous sick days, and when they do, you're the one who has to handle their work. If anything, you see more disease now than you did in the doctor's office. And, there is one more ironic kick in the pants: two weeks after you started this job, you decide to do some housecleaning. You are about to discard the job listings from which you chose your present position. One particular heading catches your eye, and you pause to read it. The listing describes a job working for a health newsletter. It offered a better salary and benefit package than you are presently earning. And the job seemed tailor made for you: they were seeking the skills you excel at, and it was a position with great potential for advancement. The position has been filled now, but it was yours for the asking. The reason you didn't notice it two weeks ago was that it was listed under Health, and you had automatically ruled out everything connected with that field.

Let's go back to your original negative motivation. As I mentioned before, your motivation, positive or negative, is the main focal point for your energy and attention. In this example, it was sick people. Instead of moving toward a job that would best employ your skills, you sought, at all cost, to avoid working with sick people. But, we draw into our life whatever we focus on, positive or negative. Since your focus was on sick people, you wound up with an office full of ailing co-workers. And an unsatisfying job.

Whenever you are faced with a change in your life, or have to make a decision, move *toward* something that you perceive to be desirable and appealing, something that will enhance your life. This is a big and dynamic world, everything is in motion, and new opportunities and situations are always opening up. If you find yourself in a position where none of the choices available to you excites your interest, do nothing. There is great power in doing nothing; it shows you have the wisdom not to be tricked into acting out of desperation. When five paths are in front of you, and they all lead to disaster, the smart thing is to choose none of them.

To be sure, we all encounter dilemmas, times when we must make a choice, and none of the options available to us look attractive. Or we may be presented with two or more alternatives, each of which has a mixture of desirable characteristics and drawbacks. Many situations do not offer us a simple and obvious choice between something that is horrible on one hand and wonderful on the other. We may encounter moments when we are thoroughly perplexed by the question, what is it that I really want?

There are two great quotations that can help us untangle our sometimes conflicting desires and sort out our motivations. By themselves, they could form the foundation for a very effective philosophy of life. In ancient Greece, above the Oracle at Delphi, were the words, "Know thyself." Centuries later, Shakespeare added, "This above all: to thine own self be true." You are a one-of-a-kind individual. Your reasons for entering into this life, your goals and aspirations, the quirks and traits of your present personality, and even the genetically coded protein structure of the body you are now inhabiting, all are unique unto you. So, while you can study all kinds of disciplines, and listen to others speak of their desires and experiences, the only way you are going to understand what makes you tick is to look within yourself.

Most people are so caught up in the demands and fascinations of the nonstop society all around them that they don't know themselves very well at all. To get in touch with yourself and regain the knowledge of who you really are, start by reminding yourself that you came here for a purpose. You have a job to do and a mission to fulfill. If you persist in this practice, a picture will begin to emerge in your consciousness, and it will become steadily clearer. Distractions and diversions that you have allowed to take up great chunks of your time will become hazy, while the image of your true task will become more sharply defined. On a summer holiday, when you have nothing in particular to do, you may dress in dungarees, slacks, or shorts; whatever suits your whim. However, if you have to appear in court, you unhesitatingly dress in formal business attire. The more you ask the question, what did I come here to do? the more apparent the answer will become.

As you get to know yourself really well, you will know what your motivations are, and why you have them. It will then be a fairly straightforward exercise to determine whether a particular motivation is positive or negative. As an illustration of how moving toward differs from moving away from something, picture a child's wagon. Let's say the wagon is on a narrow path. You want to go in one direction on that path, so you pick up the handle and pull the wagon in the direction you want to go. Now imagine that when you pick up the handle, you look down the path and say, "I don't want to go *there.*" So you start pushing the wagon away from the undesired direction. When you were moving toward a goal you wanted, the wagon followed right behind you. Now, however, as you are pushing the wagon, the wheels are out ahead of you, and you are trying to direct the whole process from behind. You have to work hard to keep the handle perfectly aligned with the wheels. With every slight variation the wagon veers to the right or the left. So, while you are moving in a general direction away from one place, you are moving erratically in several directions, and not toward any one place in particular. Now imagine how chaotic this exercise would be if you had several wagons linked together, and you tried to push instead of pull them. Have you ever observed chaotic situations, in your life or someone else's, where progress in any direction was stymied because unfocused motivation had led to inconsistent and conflicting actions? When you are motivated only by the desire to move away from something, you are liable to move in any direction, and a lot of the destinations you reach may turn out to be a good deal more unpleasant than the initial place you wanted to avoid.

So sort out your motivations. Find out what it is that you truly want, and set off in that direction. You may encounter many challenges and setbacks, but if you keep focused on where you want to go, you will continue to make choices that will advance you in that direction. Now it is helpful to remember Shakespeare's advice: "This above all: to thine own self be true." Once you know yourself, and know what your true goals and motivations are, the task is to remain true to those inner ideals. Being true to yourself means making choices that are consistent with your inner sense of purpose and identity. This adherence to your personal agenda may cause you some awkward moments whenever others will try to influence you to take a path that is not in your interests. A very simple and common situation occurs frequently when friends go out together. They are enjoying each other's company and having a good time. Then the moment arrives when the first person in the group has stayed up late enough, has had enough to drink, and wants to go home. The rest of the group wants to prolong the festivities; they will entreat and coax this person to stay out a little longer.

If this person maintains that he or she really wants to go home, the others may resort to stronger measures, pressuring and belittling the person not to be such a spoilsport and a wimp. "C'mon, stay for one more drink." Has this ever happened to you? How have you responded? If you know your body's needs and tolerances, and remain true to yourself, you will go home, get the amount of sleep you require, and be able to do what you had planned the next day. Also, the pressure, and even insults, of your friends will have no impact on you, because your own integrity, and ability to function competently, mean far more to you than their fickle opinions. The pressure to conform, to go along, to be accepted socially, weighs down upon us every day. Alienation is not a comfortable state. In the larger context, it is unnatural, because we are rooted and united in the One. All our lives we struggle with various aspects of separation. We are social beings, seeking and needing the company of others. Hence we normally shrink from anything that threatens to sever our connections to others, and we will often change or modify our behavior just so that we will not be ostracized or excluded.

Yet, conforming to group pressure and straying from our true course will invoke certain consequences, some of which may be quite costly or disadvantageous to us. For example, in the case above, if the person who wanted to go home submits to the pressure of the rest of the group and stays for one, or a couple more drinks, he would get less sleep and perhaps suffer from a hangover the following day. If this person had to go to work the next day, the hangover would adversely affect his job performance. Even if it was a weekend or a day off, he would still enjoy it a lot less and accomplish fewer things than if he were clearheaded and pain free. In more extreme cases, which occur hundreds, if not thousands, of times each year, this person, who imbibed more than he knew it was wise to drink, never made it home. Like thousands of others each year, he either fell asleep at the wheel or was so physically incapacitated by alcohol that he lost control of his car and crashed. What an awful price to pay for allowing others to override what we know is best for us.

Being true to oneself means recognizing that there are times when we have to stand alone and take a solitary path. This is not a rejection of society, but rather an affirmation that we have a mission in this life. No one can fulfill our mission for us, and certain steps along the path of our life—along the path of each person's life—must be taken alone. If we fail to take these steps, and instead retreat into the comfort of social acceptability, we will be cheating ourselves out of the life we came here to live. And, by extension, we will be shortchanging society at large by not developing and sharing those talents and abilities that were to be our unique gift to the world.

By being true to yourself you are fulfilling a bargain you made with yourself to take on this physical life. You came here with a purpose to fulfill. It's your assignment. Just as you can't do the soul work for another person, no one can take your place and travel your path for you. Within the context of the One, we are all individual souls, and the essence of being an individual is that we each have a journey of learning and discovery to make. Through self-knowledge and fidelity to who we are, we will achieve the full potential of our individuated souls. The experience, knowledge, and wisdom attained by each soul feeds back into the One Source. We are creators and creation. Remember that you are inseverably linked to everyone and everything else that exists. Being true to yourself, developing and manifesting the radiant fullness of your being, is your contribution, your way of exalting and fulfilling the All-There-Is.

Chapter Fourteen

Action Is Its
Own Reward

When you live with a full, working awareness of your eternal being, many of your attitudes and approaches to life will change. Some of the precepts that influenced your behavior in the past will no longer carry weight. Take, for example, the adage that the end justifies the means. For millennia, political and military figures, as well as the man in the street, have excused themselves from all manner of horrifying deeds by claiming that their purposes were noble, and that their long-range goal was so good that it exonerated them for whatever violence, deception, and exploitation they had to employ to reach that goal. And you would likely agree, reasoning that once a good end was achieved, one could go back and heal all the injuries one had inflicted along the way.

However, eternity goes on forever. There are no endings. In this physical world of limitations, with the very definite boundary of death facing us, it is easy to fall into the illusion that everything has a set duration, comes to an end, and that's that. This static view is very much formed and reinforced by the way we regard death. When a person dies, the animated body that moved and acted in this world stops moving, and will never speak or act again. Life is thus seen in static terms; no further changes, growth, or development will take place. We can tell the story of such a life and come to an ending, a point beyond which nothing happens. From our standpoint in this material world, we see a life as an isolated unit, and in attempting to make sense of that life or draw a lesson from it, our tendency is to see the end as the culmination, or working out, of the tactics and theories a person employed during his or her lifetime.

However, from the standpoint of eternity, nothing has truly ended. A person who dies merely crosses a boundary into another dimension and continues the journey of learning and development. The more we contemplate eternity, the more this seeming boundary of death dissolves away. As it does, our temporal view of very definite beginnings and endings begins to merge and melt into a long, unending continuum of eternal existence. Our perspective now shifts, and we see this life unbounded, as an ongoing process.

In this light, where there are no real endings, what can we now say about justifying deceptive or cruel means? From a worldview of endings, we could externalize the consequences of our actions and say that no matter what we did, it was done for the benefit of the greater society. Thus, the depravity of our actions was spread over the shoulders of the whole population, since it was on their behalf that we acted. However, since there are no real endings, only an ongoing, unending process, we are now confronted with the fact that everything we do has an internal bearing on our own soul's development. If we employ corrupt means, we corrupt ourselves. Forget about the greater good; we own our actions. The implications of what we do are reflected inward. There is no external point of finality that can somehow wash out the stain that we have painted upon ourselves. Regardless of our proclaimed righteous goals and motives, if we act in a depraved way, we are inflicting that depravity upon our own character; we are handicapping ourselves with an inner corruption. Since there are no ends to look to for justification, choose carefully the means you employ.

With the exception of death, most of us already have at least an inkling that endings are illusory. Think of some big event in your life, something that you prepared for for years. High school graduation is a good example. You study a variety of subjects and take tests and quizzes regularly for four years. All is not drudgery. There are sporting events, dances, and parties. You form a number of close friendships. Yet it all leads to one destination—final exams, then graduation. You diligently apply yourself to your studies, pass your exams, and the big day of graduation arrives. You are set apart from the crowd in your cap and gown, you receive your diploma, and your high school career ends. Now what? The world is still spinning. You get out of bed the following day and life moves on. What has really ended? The school is still there; your friends are still around. It's true that one phase of your life has reached maturity and you are now moving into a new phase. You may even reflect and realize that the graduation ceremony is called a commencement—a beginning.

There have been other occasions in your life when the work and striving of many months has culminated in a single event. Beforehand, that event looms as the summing up of everything you have done in this life. Then, the morning after the event, you get out of bed, make new plans, and do new things. Life is a process, like crossing a boundless sea. We channel our energy and actions toward attaining a certain goal; when we do, it is like ascending to the top of a wave. In that moment of attainment, we ride the crest, from which we see a succession of waves stretching out beyond the horizon. The next wave beckons, and then the one behind it. Reaching each successive summit will be a new adventure, yet we will never exhaust the sea. There will always be more waves to ride.

Realizing that our life is one never-ending process will allow us to see our goals in a new light. We usually picture a goal as a static, unchanging state. Once we reach it, we will no longer have to strive, all our questions will be answered, and everything in our life will be in its rightful place. We, too, will be in our rightful place. The world will have recognized us for the valuable and talented people we are, and will have materially rewarded us so that the rest of our lives will be filled with ease and contentment.

However, as we discussed in a previous chapter, the rational mind is a creature of habit that likes to form and maintain static pictures of ideal states where all our problems have been solved and everything is settled "once and for all." We have come to learn that these constructs of the mind are mirages. In this world, everything is constantly moving and transforming, and no one has it made. We will continue to grow, strive, and ponder new questions and mysteries forever.

Therefore, the goals that we set for ourselves are not so much end-points as they are steppingstones from which we launch ourselves into our next quest.

Even when we see our lives from the perspective of eternal beings, it is still possible sometimes to feel disappointed and shortchanged, because of the gossipy and complaining nature of our rational minds. The think-ing faculty is working all the time, chattering away about what we deserve and how we ought to be recognized and rewarded. It unceasingly makes comparisons and points out every instance where someone is being com-pensated better than we are. We've all listened to that chorus of lament many, many times: We deserve as much as so-and-so. It's just not fair!

That may well be true. This is not a fair world. Besides that, the mental reckoning of each individual is a subjective affair, and we all tend to value our output more highly than the world does. Therefore, feeling shortchanged by life is a common affliction. However, it is folly to look outside of ourselves for fulfillment. There's an old saying that virtue is its own reward. What this means is that the values of virtuous living accrue inwardly, enriching the soul. In like manner, if you want to live a full and rewarding life, bear this in mind: **Action is its own reward.**

Typically, we embark upon a course of action to reach certain goals and attain certain material rewards. Since we are creator beings, and this is a material world of abundance, with a little effort we will acquire many material goods. However, because the mind moves faster than the body, and we can rapidly expand and embellish our original desires, it often happens that those things we achieve fail to measure up to the fantastic images we have envisioned in our imaginations. Also, it often happens that, despite sustained effort on our part, we will be frustrated by factors outside of our control. Sometimes we are partially frustrated and attain only a portion of what we wanted. For instance, we may write an excellent novel that is highly praised by the critics and financially successful, yet never rises above number five on the bestseller list, even though we know it's a better story than the four books that are outselling it.

At other times, our frustration may be total. For example, a loss in an election. It is a foregone conclusion that only one candidate can be elected to any given office. Consider the contest to become President of the United States. During the election campaign both major party candidates will pour their hearts, intellects, and every ounce of energy into the race. When the election is over, the loser will have spent over one hundred million dollars, traveled tens of thousands of miles, delivered hundreds of speeches—for nothing. This person may be intellectually and ethically superior to the winner, and may have promoted more sensible policies. But the electorate chose the other candidate. How's that for frustration? Where's the fairness? Where's the reward?

Action is its own reward. In other words, our tangible rewards in this world are really only the skin on the apple. By engaging in an activity, expending our energies, using our mental and physical skills, and becoming thoroughly involved on an emotional level, we are **living.** That's what we came here to do. Living is feeling, motion, and action. Results are largely an afterthought, something to mull with our minds once the intense action has been completed. In Shakespeare's words, "the play's the thing." That is, being engaged in activity is the point of the activity.

The true benefits of our actions show up in the further development and refinement of our souls. That is where the enduring improvements are made. Each time we embark on an endeavor, and infuse it with our energy, passion, and skill, we are inwardly growing and perfecting another facet of ourselves. This continuous process of perfecting and polishing ourselves is the real reward. Wins and losses in the material world, seen from the vantage point of eternity, are of no consequence. Likewise, the temporal rewards of this world quickly fade and decay, while the refinement of our immortal soul stays with us forever.

By recognizing that our life is a process, and that the true rewards for our efforts accumulate within the subtle layers of our soul, we are free to express the best of ourselves in this world, without a concern for winning or losing. How you play the game really is the important part. We will then experience the joy and enthusiasm that comes from the unrestrained expression of our skills. Also, the act of sharing our gifts with the world will establish a momentum and take on a life of its own. One constructive act will beget another, and the quality of our open offering will attract the notice and interest of others. That which is done with energy and generosity is contagious, and others will want to share in the activity, or support it in some way. Outer rewards will often come, but the real reward is within.

Chapter Fifteen

The Perfection of Each Moment

As adults we think constantly; our heads are filled with the details of plans, projects, and activities. A basic property of thinking is that it places our focus in the past or the future. Most of our thoughts are concerned with what went wrong in the past, and what needs to be done to make things better in the future. Our attitude toward the world-as-it-is in the present moment is that everything is unfinished, insufficient, and unsatisfactory.

It was not always this way. When we were small children, we simply took in the world without feeling compelled to change or improve on it in any way. Once we entered school, we were given assignments to complete, and we began to participate in structured activities, such as sports and science fairs, where we organized materials and expended effort in the pursuit of a certain goal. At first, we were not immersed in the habit of thinking rationally all the time. We still existed more or less in the present moment. We would engage in thinking for a while and then return to a state of awareness that was essentially thought-less.

As we progressed through school, our moments of thought-free awareness steadily declined as our rational inner dialogue became more fully developed. Our activities became more complex and involving, such that they occupied our thoughts and energies whether we were in school or not. When we were in the early elementary grades, we may have had a part in a pageant, and rehearsed for it for several weeks. But we hardly gave it a thought when we were out of school. We engaged in activities while we were doing them, then largely forgot them. As we went up in grades, our concern with projects and activities became more continuous. For example, if we were on the yearbook staff or the prom committee, we thought both at school and at home about the details of what must be done.

Then we got a job. Our employment entailed duties and responsibilities, and brought with it a whole complex of interrelationships with co-workers, customers, and supervisors. Even when we were not at work, we were frequently thinking about what must be done before the next deadline.

Whereas a small child just looks at the world and sees what is there, we now look at our home, our garden, our work, and see what needs to be done. We are surrounded by works in progress. Each day we join most of the population in a mass movement to our places of work, where we are all striving to complete the unfinished business of this world. We listen to reports over radio and television, and read articles in various publications about all sorts of projects that are behind schedule, over budget, involved in litigation, and so on. We all complain and commiserate with each other that there aren't enough hours in the day for us to complete all the work that must be done. All day long we make up lists of things to do, constantly reshuffling and reordering their priorities as new demands are placed upon us and other tasks lose their relevance or urgency. It seems that everywhere we look, in our life and in the world, everything is incomplete.

Now, take a deep breath. Look out the window, scan the horizon for a moment. What I'm going to say here may be very difficult for you to swallow. Right now, in this very moment, the whole world is complete and perfect. Everything is in precisely the right place, exactly where it needs to be. I can almost hear your rational mind objecting, screaming that this project is far from finished, that such-and-such is all wrong and will have to be redone, and that some other task has barely been started. How can I state such an absurdity? The world is filled with unfinished projects.

From the perspective of our rationality, which is usually dwelling in the past or the future, it may seem that the present state is untidy and unfinished. However, *this present moment is the only one in which we exist.* We may remember the past, and imagine the future, but the present is where we are. It is where we always are. And in this present moment, everything is at a point of culmination. It has arrived at the exact point where it needs to be *in this moment.* In the next present moment, everything will have changed its position, and it will be exactly where it needs to be in that moment.

This is not an easy concept to come to grips with. How can there be change and perfection at once? It is indeed a paradox, but with a little examination and reflection it won't be so difficult to accept. Physical reality is a dynamic realm. Everything is in motion, and changing all the time. Yet, our conception of time being a dimension of extension and depth is an illusion. There is only one, eternal, present moment. There is dynamic movement within a seemingly static moment. Understand that everything is a reflection of the perfection of the Unity of All. Within the All, everything is at home, and where it needs to be. It can move and change its relationship with respect to other things, yet it is still at home, and in precisely the right place.

Think of a house being built. Imagine taking a photograph of the building site at eight o'clock each morning while construction is underway. Place all the pictures on a huge board. You will begin with a picture of the site when excavation for the foundation was begun. Successive pictures will show the foundation being poured, stacks of building materials, the frame going up, the exterior walls and roof going on, and every phase of the building, including seeding the lawn and planting shrubs and flowers. As you look at the snapshots, each picture is complete unto itself. In each one of those pictures, each item on the site is exactly where it belongs at that stage of the construction. So, at each moment along the way of the building process, everything was exactly where it was supposed to be.

Consider another example. Let's say you wanted to take a hike on a woodland trail that was five miles long. The trail begins near your house and ends at a lake, where some friends will meet you with a picnic. Along the trail, you will pass through groves of fragrant evergreens, cross over brooks in mossy, fern-filled glens, pass through stands of stately old trees in which masses of wildflowers and native shrubs will be in full bloom. You will also ascend to the top of a high ridge, where you will be treated to fine views in every direction. At every step on this journey, you will be surrounded by beauty, at peace, and at a point of culmination. There is nothing more or less perfect about the glen or the hilltop; you feel happy and content at every location along the trail.

Try to see that your life, at this moment, is at a point of culmination. All the elements of your life are where they need to be. You may not be happy with one or many issues in your life. And that is fine; you can change them. But try to understand that there is an inner logic, and an appropriateness, to the way everything fits together *in this moment.* When you begin to understand that all the comfortable and uncomfortable facets of your life are fulfilling a necessary role, you will begin to lose that sense of desperation that tells you your life is incomplete and hopelessly behind schedule. You are precisely where you need to be, in this moment.

Each moment is a culmination and, at the same time, everything is in motion. Change is taking place continually. Strange as it sounds, we exist in a state of dynamic perfection. A big key to happiness, and to recapturing the childlike wonder and joy of living, is learning to be at ease with ourselves. There will always be features of the present that we like and don't like. Not only will these features transform and change over time, but so will our likes and dislikes. Everything is circulating within a single sphere of unity.

This is the time of your life, and you have arrived. While you will continue to develop and progress, you are whole and complete right now. You are at home, and you are eternally enfolded within the All-There-Is.

Chapter Sixteen

The Work Will Always Be Here

Even though we are eternal beings, an almost universal complaint that people have in this world is that they never have enough time. We become immersed in our jobs, even if we often find the work boring and unfulfilling. Of course, we have to work; there are bills to be paid, and usually a significant amount of debt to be serviced. Beyond monetary considerations, however, we often spend more time working that we say we want to. Whether it's because we feel we are indispensable, or our notion of status and self-esteem is tightly bound to the hours and effort we expend on our jobs, many people today willingly describe themselves as workaholics: they are addicted to their jobs.

In a number of professions, long hours go with the territory. In medicine, law, and finance, twelve-hour days and longer are often the norm. Many construction and manufacturing jobs have mandatory overtime. And the majority of people who work a "normal" eight-hour day commonly spend an hour or more commuting to and from the workplace. It is also common for many people to bring work home with them: reports, plans, taxes, presentations. Even when we aren't performing the actual tasks, most of us carry our jobs home each night in the form of concerns and stress; even at home we devote a good portion of our waking attention to mulling what we will need to do and say tomorrow when we are back at work.

On the surface, we appear to have a slam bang economy. The numbers measuring gross domestic product and personal income keep rising each year. New buildings and highways are in evidence everywhere, and the shelves of the stores from coast to coast are stacked high with gleaming new products. Material abundance is everywhere. We are blessed. Under such rosy conditions, everyone should be out dancing in the streets. Why aren't we? If someone were naïve enough to go out in the streets and ask people this question, most folks would reply that they're too darn tired. And besides, they have to go to back to work tomorrow.

Beneath all the surface evidence of prosperity and well-being, there are notable signs of strain and unhappiness. Our most important relationships are not faring too well: more than half of all marriages end in divorce. Even when children are not being shuttled between separated parents, the amount of time that most families spend in each other's company is slight, and diminishing each year. Perhaps once or twice a year we will make an obligatory visit to an elderly relative, but that person's timeframe of experience, though only a couple of decades ago, bears so little resemblance to the world we are immersed in now that we seem to have very little in common to talk about.

Meanwhile, many people are experiencing a gnawing feeling that something, something big, is missing in their lives. Has it happened to you, at the funeral of a family member or friend, that you are struck with a deep regret that you didn't know this person anywhere near as well as you would have liked to have known him or her? Only when they are dead do you find out that they were accomplished in a craft or a field of study that has long fascinated you, or you recall their sense of humor which you had enjoyed so much, but all too rarely.

Have you been at the wedding of one of your children, or the child of a close friend, and realized that you only have snapshot memories of their entire childhood and maturing process? They largely grew up without you, and are now embarking on their adult life in another part of the country. They are your immediate family, yet strangers. And from this moment on you will have progressively less and less contact.

What's going on? Do you find yourself sometimes questioning what really matters in life? Of course, you have to work for a living. And your job requires long hours, because there is so much work that must be done.

Here's a very simple fact that never occurs to most people. No matter what you do, how important or crucial it may be, the world will keep spinning whether you do that work or not. And, after you're dead, the work will still be there. So many times we throw ourselves into a project, thinking that no one will do it as well or as thoroughly as we will, and that we are going to complete the task, for once and for all time. This vision may be a sweet illusion, a boost for our egos, where we are the heroic figure saving the company, and society at large, through our diligent and unstinting efforts. But it's all a mirage. Whatever work we are doing today will need to be done again, whether it's tomorrow, next week, next year, or long after we've retired and died. Or, conversely, the particular job that we have done so steadfastly for so many years will be made obsolete by technology or changing preferences in society, and no one will need to do it. In either case, our position will either be filled by someone else, or go out of fashion and disappear.

Look at any job in your community: garbage collector, lawyer, plumber, mayor, doctor, journalist, secretary, carpenter, civil engineer, teacher, etc. Go back fifty years and see if you can name anyone who held one of those positions. All of those occupations were filled a half-century ago, and a few physical remnants of the work that was done back then may still survive today. But mostly, the work that those people did was of a temporary nature, even though the tasks they performed were essential for a functioning society. Today, they have passed from the scene; and it's hard to remember any of their names. Yet there is still work, the same work, to be done.

You can work eighty hours a week, and have little or no life outside your job. You may become quite prosperous, although the number of hours you work will not translate directly into the amount of money you will make. But let's say you do well financially, and own a big house with nice furniture. With all the hours you spend at work, how much time do you have to enjoy the house and the fine furnishings in it? Do you even notice them at all? You may become a prominent citizen, so prominent in fact that a public building is named in your honor. Perhaps even a statue of you is erected in the park. But when you reach the end of your life, what will you take with you into your next existence? You can't take your money, your degrees or honorary plaques, or that statue in the park. Even your knowledge of your profession and the strategies for executing successful deals will have no applicable value in the next realm. You came here as a possession-less soul, and that is how you will leave. Your soul may be more refined and spiritually enriched from your stay here. Or it may not be. Look back over your life up to this point. In what ways and to what extent have you spiritually grown so far? Perhaps you have been putting off that sort of personal development until you became successful and, somehow, got all the work finished. But the work will never be finished. Whether at home or on the job, the mind can always find one more thing that needs doing. The rational mind is endlessly inventive, and it can always conjure up a rationale for a new project.

However, all of our projects, from assembling a jigsaw puzzle to designing a space rocket, are simply activities that we dream up to occupy those moments in between the times when we do what is really important in this life. The real work that we have come here to do is the unfolding and perfecting of our souls. That indestructible and eternal essence of ourselves, our soul, has no possessions. It doesn't need any; it is complete and whole in and of itself. Also, it has no professional designation; it is not a doer of this or that. Over many lifetimes we may engage in many activities and perform a wide variety of tasks, but we are not, in essence, a teacher, lawyer, carpenter, or musician. We simply **are.** And the highest activity we can engage in while we are on this Earth is to share our **being** with others.

Everything that we do and make is an expression of our being. Any individual can express himself or herself in an infinite number of ways. Each one of the ways we express ourselves, through music, healing arts, mechanical ability, etc., can confer a benefit to others. However, the material benefits we can produce are small change in comparison to the full, multi-faceted nature of ourselves. How do we share the entirety of our magnificent being with someone else? Simply by **being** with them. When we are in the company of another person, and drop the pretenses of professional or social roles we usually play—when we simply spend time with another person, relating to him or her as a real, whole person, we are offering the greatest, most valuable, and only gift we have—ourselves.

In this world, we are all solitary, vulnerable little beings. As part of the amnesia we took on in order to enter this world, we have forgotten our connection to everyone and everything else that exists. In truth, each of us is an individuated cell that is inextricably enfolded and rooted in the One. But in this realm, we feel separated and alienated from each other. Therefore, the greatest work we can do is to dissolve this illusion of separation and reestablish the soul-to-soul connection that physical reality obscures and disguises. To engage in this work, you don't have to **do** anything in particular. You only have to **be.** Be with another.

I know this sounds absurdly simple. But in our present-day society, it isn't. Just look back over today and tally up the minutes when you simply shared your presence, your being, with another person. Many times we shy away from such wholesome and honest, person-to-person contact. We will devise any kind of activity to maintain some form of separation. How often have you heard yourself saying, "I've got to run now; I've got to do such-and-such"?

We've all had the experience of visiting a sick friend or an elderly relative, someone who is mostly shut off from the rest of the world. When we go to see them, they don't care if we bring them flowers or candy, or if we fix the leg on their bureau. What means the most to them is our company. We don't have to do anything, in fact we don't even have to say much; what matters to their soul is that someone **be** with them.

So often we run around from one end of our life to the other, concerned about becoming someone. We forget about who we already are. We are a radiant manifestation of the Supreme Divinity. We usually cover over our radiance with degrees, assignments, and obligations. However, it requires no great deal of effort to drop these pretenses and let our splendid divinity shine through. Each time we do, we enrich the people who are in our presence. Each day we have many opportunities to engage in this work. It isn't labor intensive, and it doesn't require making or producing anything. Instead, we only have to drop the layers of responsibility and self-importance with which we usually disguise ourselves. Our greatest work is to reveal and share who we are, and let others bask in the glow of our being.

This job is deceptively simple, and yet it is the work of a lifetime. No matter how much of it we do, it will never be finished; because we are all encapsulated in our own separate bodies, so that we must constantly fend off feelings of isolation and loneliness.

At times there is great value in solitude, for it affords us the opportunity to reflect, and it is through this inner cultivation that we develop understanding and wisdom. We need not concern ourselves with racing around keeping people company all the time. The idea to bear in mind, though, is that the need is always there, and the need will persist as long as humanity in its present form inhabits this world.

Each time we share our being with another person, we are opening the door to the glorious unity that underlies physical reality. For most people, whenever they are alone, this door closes again. In this world, we are very temporal creatures. We can only hold one thought in our minds at any time, so no matter what we may have realized or experienced two minutes ago, we can be in an entirely different state of feeling and awareness in this moment. Hence, the feeling of union, and communion, we may have felt last night in the company of friends, or even ten minutes ago in the presence of one person, can now be replaced with a sensation of aloneness. We are, each one of us, vulnerable to these feelings of alienation for the entire duration of our lives. It is one of the fundamental aspects of occupying a physical body. Therefore, for each one of us, to share our presence with others is a lifelong endeavor.

The work of this world is inexhaustible. There will always be reports that need to be written, and materials to be moved from one location to another. The real value of all our labors is not the projects that get completed—they are only the visible residue of our actions. Rather, it is the enrichment of souls; and we accomplish this mission by sharing our being, our whole self, with others. If you really want to be a productive individual and true benefactor of the human race, extend company, compassion, understanding, and, yes, love to each person with whom you come in contact. Remember, each person you meet is a manifestation of the Divine Being. If you're really concerned with doing good work, offer the very best you have—your **self,** your **being.**

Chapter Seventeen
Action and Rest

There is an old Chinese saying, which goes, "When you have learned how to spend a perfectly useless afternoon in a perfectly useless manner, you have learned how to live." On first reading, most people would regard this saying as heresy. How can there be such a thing as a perfectly useless afternoon? For the last two centuries, the industrial economies have been governed by the dictum that: "Time is money." Hence, all time is useful and valuable, and it is widely deemed a secular sin to waste time.

If we equate time with money, we are saying that time is a commodity which can be divided into units of equal value. We do employ this scheme on a fairly broad basis, as most people are paid so much per hour for their labor. However, while physical commodities like boxes or nuts and bolts are equal, unit for unit, so that one box has the same value as another box of the same size and composition, the same cannot be said for time. In the case of hourly paid workers, their output of work, from hour to hour, can vary widely. Beyond numerical output, the quality of that labor can also range from superb to unacceptable. So, in the strictest sense of industrial accounting, time is not a commodity where all units are of equal value.

Beyond the workplace, we are much more subjective in our appraisal of time, in that we refer to good times and bad times. And lately we have gone so far as to say that some moments of our presence have a higher value than others. Overworked parents speak of spending "quality time" with their children, which seems to imply that the rest of the time they spend with their kids has no value or meaning at all, and it would be just as well for everyone concerned if they were more constructively occupied elsewhere-- say, at work.

If you examine your own behavior when you are at work, you will see that there are some moments when you are highly productive, and other times when you are, frankly, goofing off. Even outside of the work environment, when you are pursuing a hobby or leisure activity, you will go through daydreaming lulls and spells of focused action. So, while our puritanical training may be screaming at us never to admit such a thing, have we ever encountered a perfectly useless afternoon?

When we described a circle in the dimension of time, we had a line that moved up and down, up and down. Cyclical variations are the natural path of action through time. From this fundamental condition of the world it follows that there are times of rest and times of motion, times of activity and times of inactivity. Indeed, science has identified three distinct patterns of human activity that fluctuate regularly in cycles that range from twenty-eight to thirty-three days. They are collectively known as biorhythms. One describes the ups and downs of our emotional moods; the second, the swings in our level of mental acuity; and the third, the peaks and valleys of our physical performance. Studies have shown that people are markedly more productive and effective when their energies are on the rise, or peaking, as opposed to those times when they are on the downswing or bottoming out.

Reflect on your own experience. Have you had days when nothing you tried to do turned out right? And the harder you tried, the more things fell apart? At the end of the day, you had made no progress at all. In fact, you had hampered your projects with false starts and unnecessary complications, so that on the following day you had extra work to unravel the mess and get back to square one. At this point you may have voiced that oft-uttered lament, "I would have been better off if I'd stayed in bed!" You have just slogged your way through a perfectly use-less afternoon. Instead of fighting the rhythm and making more work for yourself, can you see that it would have been wiser to spend the time in a perfectly useless manner?

You may object that you have to work and make a living, and that you simply cannot take off for a day or two each month when your per-sonal activity cycle is heading into a trough. That is understandable. But wouldn't it be better, for you and your employer, if you could ascertain when it was favorable to press ahead and overcome obstacles in your work, and when it was more prudent to maintain your position but not try to force any issues? Look at your workplace and society in general, and observe how much work has to be redone because we are all trying to overrule the natural up and down rhythms of action and reconfigure them into an ever-ascending straight line.

For the past hundred years or so we have used the machine as a metaphor for society, the economy, and even living systems. It is a very limited metaphor, but let's use it for a moment. Looking at the body as a machine, the heart would be considered the engine. The virtue we see in machines, besides the fact that they save us a lot of heavy lifting and grunt work, is that they operate pretty much continuously. They don't sleep, get headaches, take coffee breaks, or agitate for higher wages. In our bodies, our heart pumps blood days, nights, weekends, and holidays, regardless of whether we're happy or sad, healthy or sick. From the mo-ment we're born to moment we die, the heart is at work. Yet, unlike a machine running at a steady speed, our heart isn't working constantly. It contracts to pump blood, then it rests. Throughout our lives, it follows a rhythm of pumping and resting, pumping and resting. And the fascinat-ing fact is this: it is at rest at least 75 percent of the time!

If we look at other natural systems, we will find that they also follow this pattern of short bursts of activity followed by longer periods of rest. Animals in the wild, which must fend for themselves every day, spend only a minor portion of their time finding or hunting food and eating it. The remainder of the time they are at rest. Or play. Even the weather, averaged out around the globe, has more calm periods than stormy ones. If you look at graphs of stock prices, you will see that there are brief periods when a stock will experience a high volume of buying and selling with rapid price fluctuations, followed by longer, calmer periods.

Unlike the machine model, people, animals, and living systems do not operate at a steady, continuous speed. Instead, we start and stop, move energetically, and then rest. We all encounter intervals that are perfectly useless. That is, during those times, the best and most constructive thing we can do is rest. Now, of course, you know that rest is essential for life. Whether you want to or not, you fall into bed once a day and sleep. However, our machine metaphor and accounting mentality have produced in most of us a sense of guilt concerning so-called down time, whether it is a vacation, a day off, or snippets of time here and there spent visiting or talking with people about nothing in particular, when we could be transacting more business.

Actually, there is great value in engaging in perfectly useless intervals. By doing so, we are allowing ourselves to rest. And that rest recharges us, physically, emotionally, and mentally, for our next round of activity. Also, by periodically backing away from a project and not trying to force everything to fit in a particular way, we will often gain a larger perspective and sometimes discover a better and more effective way to proceed.

As a society, we keep trying to make more and more aspects of our lives run like machines. Many stores and businesses are now open twenty-four hours a day, seven days a week. Usually, when friends meet and ask each other how they are doing, each person replies, "I'm so busy." Isn't that what you often say? And don't you hear others say it frequently? These days, people wear "busy" like a badge. It means that they're in demand, they're important, they deserve to be taken seriously, and, above all, don't dare ask them to perform any time-consuming favors.

But what does it really mean when you're busy? It means that your activities are being directed by forces outside of yourself. You are marching to an external tempo and are unable to set the agenda or the pace. Take a good look at your daily and weekly schedule. How many of your activities are things that you freely chose to do, and how many are things that you have to do? Are you self-directed, or are you being directed by others?

As members of an interdependent society, we will of course perform services for others in return for the services that they provide to us. But we need to take a hard look at the non-stop, machine-like society that we have created, and which is now running us ragged. Do you want to be a sovereign person, who sets the pace of his life and has ample time to work, play, reflect, and simply enjoy the presence of family and friends? Or are you going to race from the beginning of your life to the end, running at top speed until you can run no more? Learn to distinguish the useful from the useless. Know when to spring into action, and when to rest.

Chapter Eighteen
Death

We have already spoken about your eternal nature, and by now perhaps you have begun to consider your own immortality and to explore some of the ramifications of living forever. Yet, while we can engage in many fine visions of other worlds and dimensions that are ours to inhabit, there is one other aspect of life in this world that we rarely put into a proper perspective with our eternal life. That aspect is death, the end of our physical life and our seemingly irrevocable departure from this world.

Imagining the afterlife can be a constructive and an enjoyable pastime. But often, when the phone rings and we are informed of the passing of a close friend or relative, we are overcome with sadness, guilt, and grief. We are upset by the hard physical fact that a body, which yesterday was animated by a spirit that we loved and respected, is now cold and still. Never again will we hear that voice, see the smile on those lips or those limbs in motion, hear that laughter, or feel the loving touch and firm embrace, all of which have been inextricable portions of our own life's experiences. Perhaps this is one of those few instances in a physical life when we are able to comprehend the unity of all life. Deeply, achingly, we feel that the life which has exited from this world has torn out a portion of our own life. For there were moments, many or few, when both of our lives, and the lives of others, flowed together and commingled into one, grand overarching life in the way that many tributary streams form a mighty river. We shared moments of true communion, in happy times and sad, poured our hearts and souls into common enterprises, and, now and then, lapsed into foolish or naughty behavior. Even when we disagreed and argued, our feet still stood on the common ground that always connected us. When this person goes, everything that we shared with them now takes on a new character. Up to this point, our relationship was an ongoing, developing, and evolving thing. We had memories of times we spent together in the past, and we had the open-ended potential to extend that relationship with every word we spoke and movement we executed in each other's presence. Now, however, all motion and speech have ceased. In earthly terms, which is how we still see virtually everything, that relationship is no longer happening, no longer evolving. It is now all in the past: a completed, finished thing.

Our eternal self knows that this relationship will transform and persist. But the conscious, waking self, which is still confined to this world, is confronted with the concrete reality of termination. When we move beyond this life, we may resume all of our relationships that have been temporarily suspended by death, but that fact does nothing to ease the pain of separation that we feel right now. Here lies the corpse of someone we still wanted to talk to, and joke with, and with whom we wanted to share many more adventures in this world, in this life, *right now.*

We may also have regrets, many of them. For every occasion when you enjoyed this person's presence, there were probably three or more instances when you could not share each other's company, because of work, other commitments, or a lack of energy. We may feel guilt over arguments or ill feelings we might have directed at the deceased and for all the times we avoided the person's company, giving lame excuses because we wanted to rest or do something else. Most commonly, we feel badly because we never adequately told him or her how much he meant to us, and how much we truly did love her, warts and all. More than anything, this lack of an ideal, storybook ending plagues us.

Also, in this society, we suffer from the misconception that death is a ghastly thing, to be avoided and delayed by all means possible, for as long as possible. Every year about 15 percent of our national economy is devoted to the vain pursuit of attempting to stave off the inevitable. Medical science has now devised a number of procedures and machines that, while they don't do anything to enhance the experience of life, do extend the clinically recognized indicators that a life is still subsisting. All for a hefty fee, of course.

The fear of death stems partly from the notion that we might face a severe accounting when this life is finished, and that some, or many, of us will be sentenced to a term of agonizing retribution to atone for our misdeeds and sins. Since we've all engaged in the practice of putting off arduous or unpleasant tasks in this lifetime, it's only natural that we would want to delay the moment of reckoning in the afterlife for as long as possible, too. But the more we grow into a realization of our eternal and divine nature, the more such horror stories of hell and damnation will shrivel and fade.

However, there is another aspect of death that scares and unnerves most people. This is the idea that death is almost always a painful and agonizing process. There's a common phrase in our language: he died a horrible death. Our literature and iconography are filled with stories and pictures of people in unbearable pain and torment, beset with excruciating injuries or raging disease. With our linear way of thinking and our rational framework of cause and effect, it is natural for us to project this pain and agony onward into the afterlife. According to this scenario, the soul exits this world in a torment of suffering and goes directly into the inferno of punishment for all the transgressions, sins, and forbidden pleasures he had engaged in while on Earth. No wonder we regard death as such a disaster and tragedy.

If anything, we have blown death way out of proportion, inflating an event that is as transitory as blinking your eyes into some drawn out ordeal. Be aware of this fact: Death is merely the passage through a doorway between one world and another. While one is alive in this world, the process that leads to death may be an extended time of suffering, but **it is a part of this earthly life.** Death is the escape, the release from this earthly dimension of physical sensations that can often be painful. When a person sustains grievous injuries or succumbs to a dreadful disease, it is **this life** that becomes horrible and unbearable. Death is the exit door.

Again, all of our conceptions about life, experience, and sensation come from what we have known in this physical world. We have forgotten what a spiritual existence feels like, if it feels like anything at all. Because the spiritual frame of reference is so completely different from the material frame of reference, we are at a loss, while we are in this world, to comprehend how one exists, experiences, and feels without a physical body to absorb and record all of the sensations. But this is an immense universe, and there are many, many ways of existing and being that we can't even imagine with the limited resources of the physical brain. The point to reflect on here is that death is not a painful or terrifying event, nor is it a gateway into a realm of punishment. The material dimension, where we feel many forms of physical discomfort and pain, where we endure the anguish of doubt and the agony of separation and rejection— this place is hellish enough.

In a number of cultures that live more within the rhythm of the seasons, and the cycles of birth, growth, and death, there is a fuller and calmer understanding of this process. Among some tribes of Australian Aborigines, a person has two parties in their life. The first is at birth, to welcome him or her into the world. The second is at the end of life, before death. At the second party, each member of the tribe tells the person how much they appreciated him, what they learned from him, and how they enjoyed his personality and his company. After this grand sendoff, the person retreats to a private place and lets the spirit slip out of the body.

What we need to do in our society is remove all the elements of melodrama and soap opera from death. All too frequently we focus on the final suffering, the last gestures and words, as if these were the most profound, important, or meaningful things the person ever said or did. We also sometimes indulge in an almost ghoulish fascination with the physical details of illness or injury that led directly to the termination of the life. A final illness, or life-ending injuries, only serve as a vehicle to transport the person from this dimension to the next one.

Think of it this way: You are about to embark on a fabulous trip overseas. You will be visiting lands you have never seen before, having adventures with exotic and fascinating people, and engaging in all kinds of wonderful new experiences. All expenses have already been paid, and you're in perfect health. A taxi takes you to the airport. Do you bother to notice the color of the cab, or if the fenders are clean? Heavens, no. You're too excited about your trip. Begin to look at death the same way. It is but a momentary, painless transition.

There is another aspect of the way we regard death that causes us much grief. It has to do with our feelings that a person's death was untimely and could have been prevented or held off for a while longer. This attitude is entirely self-centered. From *our* point of view, the person should have lived longer. But who are we to make such a determination? That life did not belong to us; its mission and tasks were not ours.

Picture someone standing before a maple tree in the autumn, pronouncing when every colorful leaf on the tree should fall. Can you see how ridiculous he would look, racing to and fro, admonishing individual leaves, "You're not supposed to drop yet, go back to your branch!" Or trying to hold back or redirect the wind so that it wouldn't upset his schedule by sweeping away thousands of leaves prematurely? We would laugh and say, "Presumptuous fool! Who does he think he is?" Well, who do we think we are, to intervene in the course of another person's life?

The moment when an individual life is ripe and ready for transition is not for us to know, and certainly not for us to determine.

It is a virtue to be helpful, but that virtue becomes twisted when we seek to be heroic, to mold and shape events that are none of our business. When we are helpful, we contribute our skill and energy in the service of another person's need, at his request and with his permission. When we seek to play the hero, our ego takes command of the stage, and we will move heaven and earth to save the day, even when our efforts are not wanted and result only in more suffering.

In our approach to death, we must separate our loving concern and compassion from the ego-driven urge to be the hero in someone else's drama. We are all going to die: that is, pass out of this world. A portion of a funeral oration given by Big Elk in 1815 states, "Death will come, and always out of season." Yes, for us, who are left behind on this earthly plane, the departure of a loved one will always seem to be too early. However, this earthly life is merely a single brush stroke on a very large canvas. When you look at a finely executed painting, every element is in its proper proportion, every brush stroke is of the right length. Trying to unnecessarily prolong or extend a life would be like extending the Mona Lisa's exquisitely enigmatic lips into a silly smile.

Even in sudden, accidental, and tragic circumstances, the death is timely—for that person. Like every other instructive instance, death carries lessons for us to learn. A single death can convey a multitude of lessons. The simple act of reflecting back on someone's life can bring to mind the qualities that he embodied, and the ideals she espoused. From her example, we can garner lessons in how to conduct our affairs, and even receive cautionary lessons in how not to behave. Remember also that the person who has departed this life is still conscious, aware, and learning. The circumstances of her death can often teach her a profound truth that had eluded her all her life. When you are six years old you are capable of operating a little toy car, which is almost an exact replica of a full-sized automobile. Yet no one would be foolish enough to hand you the keys to the family car and send you out on the interstate highways. In the same way, there are certain lessons that we are not mature or seasoned enough to grasp until we are twenty years old. Or thirty. Or forty. Or eighty. And there are certain things that we might not be ready to learn until we are in the transition state between this world and the next. The less we try to force the world to conform to an image that our ego says is the way the world ought to be, the more we will be able to learn and experience what really is. And we will save ourselves a lot of grief and hurt feelings.

In a similar way, we should not become all overwrought about our pets, with regard to prolonging or saving their lives. It can be especially hard to lose a pet. Often, we will bond much more closely to a cat or dog or other animal than we will to our fellow humans. This practice is understandable when you observe that society sanctions the unreserved expression of affection for pets in a way that it does not for other people, except very little children. If an animal wanders off, disappears, or is abducted, his absence is painful enough. But we can also put ourselves through tortures of guilt that we should have prevented this occurrence in some way. It is helpful to keep in mind that while you may think you own an animal in the sense of purchasing him at a pet store, this is only a transparent invention of the rational mind. You may have a pet for a dozen or more years, but you do not own its life. Yours is the only life you own. Whether it is a pet, a relative, or your best friend, each life must pursue its own destiny.

Bear in mind also that you can develop a profound and deep understanding and acceptance of death, and yet, when someone close and dear to you dies, you will still feel the pain of separation acutely. When we revel in someone's presence, it is natural that we will miss him, and long for him, when he departs. This pain of separation hints at the true quality of our being; for our souls are joined in unity with every other soul. Within our deepest consciousness we are always aware of this unity. But the physical fact of separation in this world contradicts our inner knowing. Since our waking consciousness cannot step outside of the confines of the illusion we call physical reality, we are jarred and hurt by this seeming contradiction.

At such times, it is good to reflect on our eternal natures, and to remember that our departed loved one is eternal, too. Everything persists; nothing is ever lost. Earthly life is like a party where some of the guests go home earlier than others. However, the underlying strands of unity that connect us with one another are never severed.

Chapter Nineteen
Death (continued)

Each one of us has a distinct path to follow through life. We all have our individual agendas to pursue and specific tasks that are ours, and ours alone, to tackle. For each individual, there are many, many ways to live. You can live an abstemious, monastic life, or you can be a libertine, chasing after every possible sensual pleasure. Depending on your choices and your physical constitution, you may enjoy vigorous health, or you may be sickly, debilitated, and plagued with multiple ailments. All paths are possible. Although you chose some general directions before you were born, the specific avenues you take depend on your desires, intentions, and day-to-day choices. Along each path there are lessons to be learned. With great vitality you can learn fine things and accomplish a great deal. You can also learn profound lessons through illness and physical handicap. Whatever your condition, you can derive great instruction if you open up your awareness to the causes of that condition, its workings, and how it relates to other states of health and disease. If you are ill, the tendency is to clench one's fists and resist and deny the disease. If, instead, you immerse yourself in the experience of the disease so that you can see the road by which you arrived at this state, it will be that much easier to see the road back out again. Through experiencing an illness and coming to know its consequences and effects, we can gain a fuller understanding of the processes of earthly life. We can also develop a deeper feeling and compassion for others who are afflicted. By paying attention to what makes us ill, we can also learn what to do and what not to do to stay healthy.

Our path through life is different from everyone else's, right up to the instant of our death. We might say that there are millions of ways to die. Actually, this is something of a misstatement, and it leads us into a lot of dread and anguish. Truly, there is only one way in which we die. We die when we separate from the physical body and step over the threshold into non-material existence. In contrast, the process of dying—that is, the path we take to arrive at this threshold—is infinitely variable. For some people, the path is exceedingly short: being struck by a bus, or suffering a massive heart attack. For others the path is a little longer, or perhaps much longer. Some people may experience a short illness, like pneumonia. While others may decline slowly for months, even years, with cancer, heart disease, or other wasting conditions. What we need to realize here is that each individual way of dying is a course of instruction. It offers lessons not only to the person whose life is ending, but also to that person's family, friends, and caregivers. There are more lessons in this world than we can absorb in one lifetime. Yet it is to our eternal advantage to be receptive to as many lessons as possible. The more we learn, the more we grow and unfold as a multifaceted jewel in the universe.

From the perspective of the individual who is dying, his final chapter of earthly life may offer him time to reflect on the choices he made in his earlier years, and the consequences of those choices. It can be a time of great realization and understanding, and an opportunity to make peace with one's past. It can also be a time of confusion, frustration, and intense suffering, yet even these hardships can broaden the soul's understanding of the interplay between the eternal energy of the soul and the constraints and obstructions presented by material reality. It is important for some people to travel the full circle from material dependency as an infant, through a life of independent, effective living, and back again to a state of utter physical dependency, not able to feed or dress themselves.

What could one possibly learn from such an embarrassing state of helplessness? For one thing, connection to society, and beyond that, to the underlying unity of All-There-Is. None of us step into this world as an independent, unaided entity. First, two people must come together to initiate the physical vessel that we will occupy. Then, our mother diverts sustenance from her own physical economy to grow our infant body and birth it into the world. In our early years, we are unable to fend for ourselves, and are protected and nurtured by our families. Throughout our lives, on more occasions than we can remember, and in more ways than we might care to acknowledge, we have been helped over the rough spots by friends and by the kindness of strangers. In our adult years, many of us forget just how vulnerable and fragile our physical vessel is. We may be successful in our profession, but fail to remember the people who gave us those crucial breaks that allowed us to establish our careers. We may even indulge in the arrogance of thinking that we are entirely self-made, and that our contribution to society is of higher value than most other people's. In this way we downplay the worth of others and diminish, in our eyes, the extent of our reliance on the services of others. A debilitating illness in our later years may knock us off the pedestal of importance on which we have installed ourselves above the majority of our contemporaries. The person who feeds us and empties our bedpan now becomes a much more important and valuable individual in our estimation. For some of us, this is a necessary lesson to learn before exiting this life.

Alternatively, we can consider a person in a similar situation but whose loss of independence results from diminished mental capacity. Remember the years of early childhood, when the whole world was fresh and new. It was a wondrous time, but we had to grow up, go to school, get a job, raise a family, and contend with all the thousands of adult issues and concerns that society throws at us. We may faintly remember one or two happy and special moments from our early childhood, but we have too many pressing, grownup demands on our attention and energy. Our days are crammed full of thoughts regarding assignments, deadlines, bills, taxes, conflicts, and competitors. The years pass, and eventually we retire. In our later years, it is no longer necessary to keep up to date with world events. Since we're no longer working, new developments in our former field of employment are now of little or no interest to us. We no longer have pressing problems to think about all day. One by one, those things that concerned or interested us fade in importance and lose their compelling quality. The mind relaxes, and the thinking process slows. Gradually, we become more child-like, more short term in orientation, and more open to the wonder of ordinary things and occurrences. For some people, this transition into a dependent child-like state is actually an opportunity to return to the realm of wonder they briefly experienced from ages one to four. Only now they may occupy it for several years, and they are able to revel in the magical aspects of the everyday world as only those who are carefree can. For decades, they shut out this aspect of the world because they had deadlines to meet, budgets to stay within, adversaries to keep at bay.

Of course, not all paths leading to the doorway of death are fun or tranquil. Disease, frustration, and regret can plague many people's final hours, months, and years. In each case, the experience has a great deal to teach. Some people learn endurance and patience, some learn forgiveness, and some review their past mistakes and use them to formulate new plans for how they will do things differently in their next material existence.

It is not just the person dying who can derive great lessons from this process. Everyone around the person can also come away from the event with new knowledge and understanding. When we witness the last days of a loved one who is suffering from an incurable disease, we can receive valuable instruction in how to exhibit grace and humor in the face of difficult circumstances. Many times people are at their best when conditions are at their worst, and the example they give to others can have a profound and long-term effect. Also, in caring for one who is deathly ill, we may find ourselves in the position of having to reach deep within ourselves to extend patience, compassion, and service that we did not think we possessed. In some cases, the prolonged suffering of a dying person is actually their gift to those around them, because it provides the family the opportunity to exhibit cooperation, forgiveness, and caring behavior that they all too often shut away when there is no crisis.

There are instances where a dying person will use the occasion to wring out of their family and friends devotion and proofs of loyalty and affection that they may feel they did not receive enough of while they were alive. Some people use their demise to extract promises from family members that will ensure that their wishes are still being followed long after they are in their grave. In such a case, what is the lesson to be learned? For the survivors, it may be learning the proper balance of honor for a loved one versus living in one's own integrity and not allowing oneself to be manipulated and controlled, especially through a twisted sense of loyalty and guilt.

Everything that we experience in this world, even the events leading up to our death, conveys profound information to us. It is full of meaning that we can use to expand our awareness and deepen our understanding.

One final word here. It may not properly belong in a section dealing with death. It is a feeling that crops up often in our lives, although we may feel it in an especially acute sense when we think about the overall course and sweep of our lives. That is the idea of wasting time, or, in its more maudlin aspect, of wasting one's entire life.

We are creatures that are very much affected by stories. The world is full of stories: myths, novels, plays, and movies are just a few examples.

Every day, in our course of interacting with other people, we listen to their stories and in turn tell them stories of our own. Most significantly, in the internal dialogue that runs almost incessantly in our brains, we are telling ourselves stories. Mostly, we tell ourselves the story of our own lives; how it ought to be, and how it's going to be when we get all the elements in order. However, the way our life works out rarely matches the story of how we said it was going to be. We engage in activities that are not successful, relationships turn sour and end; our path leads us into many false starts and dead ends. This was not the way it was supposed to be. Our life did not follow the script we had written for it. And so we sometimes feel discouraged and believe that our time and energies have been wasted.

First, it is important to understand an essential feature about stories. Almost without exception, they have been extensively corrected, revised, rewritten, and edited. What we read, or see on a stage or screen, is a final version that has had all the false starts and pointless meanderings removed. Even the tales and anecdotes that people tell to us, and that we tell to others, have been edited into a form where they come to a point; they reach a conclusion, a punch line. The structure of all stories is that they have a beginning, a middle, and an end. Our life is not like that. As eternal beings, we have no end; and it's even hard to pinpoint any sort of a beginning. Stories can be useful metaphors to illustrate various qualities and aspects of life, but they are a pale construct when placed beside the real thing. Stories may describe this or that portion of a life; they may approximate certain dynamics of a relationship and the feelings one has, but they are not life. To keep an audience's interest and to satisfy the rational faculty that fuels their interest, a story must proceed along a logical path to some sensible conclusion. In life, the illogical and non-rational play just as big a part in our development as does logic. Perhaps bigger. We suffer, needlessly, when we try to incorporate non-rational episodes into the rational, step-by-step narrative of our life-as-it-ought-to-be. Our rational faculty, along with the accounting mentality, insist that each action and every moment must fit into the logical framework of advancing the hero of the story toward the ultimate goal. Any dalliance, any wandering down a blind alley, any failure, are thus regarded as errors to be edited out of the story. Because it did not move the hero forward toward the goal, it was a waste—of time, effort, resources, and life itself.

Editing is a fine device for trimming down a story and getting it to make logical sense, but life works differently. The function of our life is to gain experience. And all experience has value—pleasure and pain, anger, sadness, elation, embarrassment, joy, melancholy, happiness, regret—we are here to fill our baskets with flowers of all sizes, shapes, and colors. We become disappointed when the logical story that we have fashioned for how our life ought to be does not match the life we actually live. The story is the edited version, the way we would like to portray our heroic self to others. Our life is the full experience, and while our rational, accounting faculty may not want to own up to foibles and failures that have littered our path, each one of them has actually been an integral building block in our life. We must shift our attitude away from the notion that this life is supposed to culminate in one grand climactic moment, like the end of a movie. This life is just one episode in a never-ending adventure, and each dalliance, each false start, each disastrous failure, has taught us great things about ourselves and about this dimension of reality. In this light we see that nothing has been wasted after all. Even times of listlessness and dissipation have taught us lessons that we needed to learn. If we now regard certain periods of our life, when we remained too long in a negative situation or a defeatist frame of mind, as a waste because we should have left the situation or thrown off the attitude sooner, the best response is just to laugh and acknowledge that we are a stubborn, slow, learner. We're the ones who determine how fast or slow we progress. Each one of us learns and unfolds at our own pace.

Take heart in the knowledge that nothing is ever wasted. Each one of us has spent years in jobs, relationships, and enterprises that did not work out well in the long term. The rational tendency is to think that because, in our opinion, things turned out wrong, all those years and effort were wasted. However, put aside the rational construct of stories that have a beginning, middle, and end. We are eternal beings, and our souls are forever unfolding. In this context, even when things may turn out wrong, we are simply taking another step in the process of learning how to get it right.

Chapter Twenty

Reincarnation and Karma

Imagine walking into an unlit room at night. It is pitch black. Suddenly, someone shines a light in your eyes. The light is so bright that it commands all of your visual ability. You are in a room, but you have no idea how big it is, and whether it is furnished or not. The only thing that registers in your eyes is that bright light. Physical reality is like that. It grabs our consciousness so powerfully and commands our attention so fully that it is virtually impossible to discern all the other dimensions that exist around us.

Throughout this book I have repeatedly referred to those aspects of ourselves that are eternal and extend beyond this world, both temporally and spatially. While the whole universe is accessible to us, this earthly realm is particularly fascinating and compelling. So much so that we may choose to come here many, many times.

Living more than one physical life involves the notion of reincarnation. Some people may be put off by this idea, but it's no big deal. To begin with, lets look at the word itself. The root of this word comes from the Latin adjective *carnal,* which means, of or pertaining to the body or flesh. An *incarnation* is the bodily manifestation of a life force, such as yourself. The act of joining your spirit with a material, fleshy body and being born into this world is an act of *incarnating.* It is something you have done already. Do you remember doing so? Do you remember the moment of your birth? Probably not. From your perspective at this moment in your life, it was no big deal. Taking on a fleshy body and being born is merely the doorway into this physical realm where you can work with tangible objects and have material experiences. In the same way, death is the exit door where you remove the outer garment of the body and return to a spiritual dimension.

What inspired you to come here in the first place? There are numerous features about the physical dimension that are inviting and enticing. You may have been inspired with a desire to visit this world in order to dance and sing, and smell the flowers. There are also the challenges of dealing with opposing forces and wrestling with physical matter, and you may have been seized with a compelling sense of purpose to have the visceral experience of working in intimate, and often arduous, contact with this hard/soft, wet/dry, cold/hot, material stuff. As a creator being, you may have come here to actualize buildings, sculpture, mechanical designs, teddy bears, or any one of the millions of manifested marvels that humans have fashioned on this planet. There are an infinite number of activities and projects to engage in on this material plane of reality.

Alas, the length of any individual incarnation is pretty short. It is easy to draw up a long list of all the meaningful and wonderful things you would like to accomplish in a lifetime, before you actually enter into the life. However, just as right now it is almost impossible for you to imagine a dimension that is timeless, prior to your birth it is just as difficult to allow for all the distractions and frustrations of this world that will prevent you from completing all of the tasks you set for yourself. Even in this world we know how that process works. How many things did you want to get done last weekend, and how many of them did you actually do? It is very common, almost universal, to look back at the end of life and wish that we had had more time, more opportunity, or better luck, so that we could have achieved more of the goals and completed more of the tasks that we had assigned for ourselves in this lifetime that is about to end. Whatever your age, look back in your life right now. Do you recall projects that you wish you had finished, relationships that didn't develop as fully as you had wished they would, words said in anger that you would like to take back, arguments you wish you had resolved? No one has a perfect trip through this life. Yet don't you feel that you could have lived this life at least a little better than you did? That you could have made some better choices, worked a little more efficiently, behaved a little more kindly and wisely? It's too late to go back and rectify all the mistakes and things that didn't go well in the past. However, if you had another chance, if you could take the knowledge and wisdom from the hard-won lessons you learned this time around and apply it to a new life, would you do it? Aren't you just the slightest bit curious to know what your life would have been like if you had continued with your piano lessons and become a performer, or if you had followed your heart and apprenticed yourself to the woodcarver in your neighborhood instead of going to college and becoming an accountant? You made certain choices and lived a particular life. But there are so many paths to follow, so many different and intriguing lives to live in this world. Do you feel a yearning well up inside you to be able to come back to this banquet of earthly life and sample some of the delectable dishes that you had no room to fit onto your plate this time?

If you know what it is like to feel even the slightest stirrings of that yearning, you will begin to understand how a soul that was once embodied, or incarnated, would want to return and *re-incarnate* to try new endeavors, or to pursue goals that weren't attained in a previous life.

At this point, again remember that you are eternal. Your existence goes on forever and ever. For most of us, the life we are living right now is the only one we remember, and if we have any conception of an afterlife, it is usually framed in the terms of being a punishment or reward for what we have done in this one life. This is a completely static picture, and if you mull the limitless extent of eternity for a while and then return to this picture, you will see how utterly absurd it all seems. Once you stop looking at the spiritual dimension and the afterlife in static terms, and realize that you will continue to learn and develop and have new experiences, both happy and challenging, then the idea of recurring visits to physical reality becomes much more plausible. Keep in mind that, as an eternal being, you didn't spring into existence at the instant of your birth. You have already experienced many lives in many different forms and dimensions.

One discomforting thing for some people when they consider reincarnation is that they are so strongly focused on the ego identity of who they are today that it is exceedingly difficult to imagine that they could inhabit a different body, with a different name, a different face, and even different personality traits. Our attachment to our present ego is so firm that we have lost sight of the fact that this ego personality is something we have acquired for the duration of this one life. The ego of course will protest, and we will usually go along with this resistance, because we have become very comfortable in our present personality; being stripped of it looms as a threatening or frightening prospect. Without this set of familiar, personal traits by which people know us, and by which we feel that we know ourselves, who are we?

It requires a certain measure of reflection and insight to begin to realize that our eternal soul, which is unique, full of life, and marvelous, has adopted our present ego in the same way that an actor assumes the part of a character in a play. As Shakespeare put it so well, an actor, in his lifetime, will play many roles. With just a brief look over the past few years we can enumerate a series of different parts we have played: supportive parent, diligent worker, crusading citizen, angel of mercy to the sick, intransigent cheapskate to a desperate salesman, humorless curmudgeon to the neighborhood pranksters. All of the qualities we develop and exhibit over the course of a life blend and meld together into the unique expression which is our ego personality. This personality has been influenced and shaped by our family background, our education, our work experience, and our personal relationships, as well as our inner drives, ambitions, fears, and preferences. In another lifetime, with a whole different set of external influences, and different inner goals and lessons to pursue, we will develop a completely different ego personality. The easier it becomes for you to view your present ego as a role you have taken on, the easier it will be to accept the idea that you can, when this role has run its course, exchange it for another one.

All too often when people think about reincarnation, they become wrapped up in fanciful speculation about which famous or important person they may have been in an earlier life. Such thinking is mired in the superficial concerns of a gossipy rationality. It misses the deeper issues of why a soul would choose to return to physical reality. A famous life is often not particularly happy. Also, with fame, a person tends to become distracted by, and involved in, the empty show of public drama, with few opportunities for quiet reflection and inner learning.

Many times, the lives that are lived quietly and humbly are the ones in which the soul learns great lessons and develops wisdom. Again, one of the framework features of this physical realm is the amnesia that obscures our memories of the other physical incarnations we may have had, as well as the immense totality of our larger soul. Compared with eternity and infinity, the human brain is a very tiny, limited instrument. It is adequate for managing the affairs of a single life that is encapsulated within the boundaries of time and space. But a full knowledge of all of the soul's memories and experiences would literally overload the brain's circuits. This amnesia serves the very constructive purpose of keeping our focus fixed on the specific lessons and experiences that are the purpose of the present life.

Depending on the individual soul, one may develop a stronger or weaker attachment to physical reality, as well as to that particular expression of material life that is known as humanity. Keep in mind that the entire universe is at our disposal. So is the entire earth. With my own limited memory in this lifetime, I cannot describe to you the variety of experiences and types of lessons one would learn from a lifetime spent as an oak tree. Or a tiger. Or a housefly. However, each living being in this world is also here on an adventure of discovery and development. It is a conceit of our rational minds that we consider them "lower" forms of life. We are looking at the world through the filters of our human perspective. How the world is apprehended by dolphins, which can communicate simultaneously over several different frequencies, I cannot say. Whether the level of their awareness, or the awareness of any other life form, is above or below that of humanity, I don't know. The awareness of humanity, with the exception of a handful of mystics, cannot tap into the awareness of other species and apprehend the way they experience life. Yet, I can say that each species of life is here for a definite purpose, and that each species experiences life in a unique way, so that an entity could spend a lifetime in each species in order to round out its understanding of all the nuances of physical experience that were offered on this particular planet.

Perhaps we should step back for a moment and look at you, a divine soul on a journey of discovery and experience throughout the infinite extent of multi-dimensional reality. The entirety of all that exists is open to you. There are more dimensions, levels, and modes of existence than the human mind can imagine, let alone count. And reality itself is not a static affair, either. It is constantly evolving, unfolding, and creating new forms, new dimensions, new universes. You and I are not just passive observers of all this activity. We are integral parts of this creative process. Through our imaginations, we bring new forms, devices, and worlds into being. Look at all the new life forms, landscapes, and dimensions that artists, inventors, writers, musicians, and filmmakers have conjured up in just the past few years. In a similar and very real way, we are also engaged in the creative work of expanding reality and bringing new worlds and dimensions into being.

See yourself as an adventurer who spans the breadth of the universe. You are driven by a desire to understand the most minute workings of this world, while also comprehending every force and object that makes a galaxy function. Your scope of personal experience ranges from the subatomic to the galactic, and beyond. Much of your activity takes place in various subtle realms of the spirit.

Not all entities choose to enter into the dense dimensions of physical reality. But you have, because you like a stiff challenge. And this world, with its nose-skinning, concrete limitations, is a demanding challenge indeed. While some entities never enter into physical reality, others may pop in for a lifetime or two, satisfy their curiosity or have their fill of it, and move on. There are some, however, who get hooked on the challenge. As discussed earlier, you almost never live a perfect life in this material world. Plans go awry, we don't attain our goals, relationships go sour, and we come to the end of our earthly life with a long list of regrets and disappointments. That's okay. You came here for the experience of life in this dimension, and the pains and travails are just as valid as the successes and triumphs. Often, in fact, we learn more from our defeats than we do from our victories. Yet still, when we have immersed ourselves in rational thinking, which divides and compares and keeps score, we can get caught up in the notion of wins and losses, and we can develop a strong yearning to experience a physical life where we get everything, or nearly everything, right, where the scorecard at the end of our life shows that we were a big winner.

Consider the game of bowling. It is possible to attain a perfect score of 300. All you have to do is bowl twelve strikes in a row. Let's say you bowl a game, and your score is 176. You succeeded in converting several spares, and even rolled a few strikes. Yet you know you could have done better. So you bowl another game. This time your score is 192. A further improvement, but not perfect. Still, you rolled a few more strikes on your second outing. And you know you can refine your technique and score higher. You bowl another game. And another. You become an avid bowler, and participate in three different leagues each week. Over the course of a year, you bowl several hundred games. In each league you maintain a respectable average in the mid 200s. You have bowled over 280 on five occasions, but that perfect game remains out of reach. Still, you press on. In your bones you know it's just a matter of time before you attain perfection and bowl twelve strikes in a row.

You may keep up this pace, bowling several times a week, for twenty years or more. While you may get very close, you might never achieve that 300 game. You have progressed through the ten frames of a game thousands and thousands of times, yet you still look forward, eagerly, to your next opportunity to bowl. Throughout the years you have had many happy times on the lanes, shared a lot of jokes, won some big matches. There have also been times when you have been off your game and suffered humiliation and defeat. Through it all you have learned a great deal, both about the external aspects of bowling, such as body coordination, proper shoes, and the various ways the maintenance crew waxes the floor. You have also gained a great deal of inner knowledge about personal motivation, perseverance, confidence, and the inevitable ebb and flow of one's fortunes. Some days you win, some days you lose.

You may never roll that 300 game. Or, let's say a day comes when everything feels exactly right, and in your first game of the night you bowl nothing but strikes. What happens now? Would you put down your bowling ball and walk out of the lanes, never to return again? Or would you press on, first to see if you could score a second perfect game in a row? Or failing that, to see how many more consecutive strikes you could add to your string of twelve? Beyond that, you're also in line to have your highest ever three-game series. Wouldn't you like to garner that triumph as well?

As you can see, an involvement with the game of bowling can become quite a habit. In fact, it can become addictive. Look at yourself, your friends and acquaintances, and you will notice that most people have one or more hobbies or activities that they will do whenever they get the opportunity, something to which they are obsessively devoted and can never get enough of.

Some pursuits are endlessly challenging. It is not perfection we are striving for, but the thrill and fulfillment that come from engaging in the activity. Such an understanding was well expressed by Thomas Jefferson, who, toward the end of his life, wrote to a friend, "I am an old man, but a young gardener."

Life in physical reality is like that. There are so many challenges and variables that, no matter how well we perform in one lifetime, there is always room for improvement. And a big component of each soul's journey is a quest for improvement. In this light, reincarnation will be seen to be a perfectly sensible procedure. From one lifetime to another, the soul will seek to build upon the knowledge and understanding that it accumulated in the previous life or lives, as well as to complete tasks that were either frustrated or beyond the scope of a single lifetime.

At this point you may be wondering about mistakes and transgressions a person has committed. There is the whole notion of *karma*, the atoning, or repayment, for one's improper acts in a past life. All too frequently people have imagined karma in very rigid, mechanistic terms: such as, if John punched Harry in this life, Harry will punch John in the next life. Our rational faculty tends to see everything in linear, simplistic terms, which, as usual, misses most of the picture. First, instead of the word *karma,* let's use the term atonement. Broken up into its constituent parts, the word is *at-one-ment.* Therefore, atoning means restoring to wholeness, to the fundamental unity where all is equal, and all is one. When people engage in disagreements, conflict, and violence, separations and disparities are created. In the ultimate fulfillment of our souls, all is healed, and everything that has been fractured is made whole again. This restoration to a whole-some state is the process of atonement. Now this universe is a huge, open-ended system. There are a multitude of ways to achieve an objective. When it comes to righting a wrong, healing a hurt, there are many ways to proceed.

Instead of thinking of karma as specific situations or actions, think of it as a process. Edgar Cayce, in his past-life readings, gave numerous examples of straight line, cause and effect types of karma. In one instance, a person who, as a Roman soldier, had blinded his prisoners, was now living a life as a blind person. Fair enough; that is one possible path. It would be just as appropriate for that person to live a life as an optometrist. Or as a researcher investigating herbal remedies that strengthen eyesight. The concept to keep in mind is that of restoring balance.

Transgressions committed in this dimension need not even be atoned for here; they can be rectified on another plane of reality. However, it is part of the overall lesson of existence, in which we are all part of the universal unity, that we will repair and restore that which we have broken or injured, one way or another. Looked at in this way, you can take comfort in knowing that there is justice in the universe. All debts will eventually be paid. All rifts will be healed. All that has been broken will be mended and made whole.

The accounting facet of the rational mind tends to keep a tally of who has hurt or cheated us, and by how much. Human society devotes way too much attention to assessing blame and seeking compensation and retribution. Instead of being concerned with how much others owe us, we need to look within and focus on the work we need to do. We have all been unjust and unkind. The place to begin creating a society characterized by integrity and fairness is with ourselves.

All too often we concern ourselves with how others are going to atone for their transgressions. More or less, we all lapse into a victim mentality. From the depths of our pain, we know how profoundly we have been injured, and who is at fault. We devote a great deal of our mental and emotional energy to devising scenarios in which the guilty party will pay the full price for his or her sins. And this is not simply a mental exercise. The courts of nations worldwide are clogged with lawsuits in which one aggrieved party is seeking both compensation and punitive damages from another party that has injured, cheated, or exploited the victim. But we need not worry about righting all wrongs in this temporal world. The All-There-Is embodies the totality of reality and will effortlessly, without prejudice, malice, or indignation, even all scores and balance all accounts. All debts will ultimately be paid. The only pertinent ones that should concern us, therefore, are the ones we owe to others.

From this perspective, we can step outside the idea that a person with some particularly nasty affliction is paying for his ghastly sins of a previous life. Thinking in this way only reinforces the vindictive and judgmental attitudes of the rational faculty. A person who is paralyzed or deformed may be on an adventure to explore the full implications and possibilities of learning how to function with such a handicap, in a similar way that runners will practice with weights on their legs to build up their muscles and stamina. Also, seriously afflicted people often perform a great service to the rest of humanity by presenting us with a concrete opportunity to extend ourselves in compassionate and generous ways that would not be called upon if everyone were perfectly healthy.

Living in this world draws forth the imperfections in us all. It is easy to react with anger, peevishness, or resentment when someone or something impinges on our comfort zone and forces us into a space that is painful, threatening, frightening, or simply entails hard work. In each moment we can react in a positive, life-affirming way or, ruled by our discomfort and sense of injury, we can seek to divide, ostracize, and punish. Remember that everything you think, feel, and do ripples out energetically. It interacts with and produces effects upon all of the energetic emanations that are being produced by everyone else in the world.

Try to picture all the emanations you produce as creating an edifice, which is the shape of all the emotions and energy you project out to the world, as well as your actions. You construct this edifice continually over the course of all your incarnations. It can have any shape, and the shape that it takes grows directly out of your attitudes and actions. From one side to the other, top to bottom, it may be out of proportion due to vanity, intolerance, greed, or cruelty. The process of karma, or atonement, is the gradual reshaping and smoothing of all the hard and unbalanced edges until it conforms with the physical representation of harmony and unity, the sphere.

Chapter Twenty-One
Money

One of the shortest chapters in this book will deal with the topic that is the central concern of most people—money. I have already stated my belief that the whole discipline of economics is founded upon a fallacy. Namely, the myth of scarcity.

We possess astoundingly creative capabilities. And, contrary to the way it sometimes appears, this is an infinitely malleable and adjustable world. One hundred years ago, who would have thought that we would be able to use the main component of sand, silicon, as a substrate for all the microscopic circuits that power the computer chips that direct the functions of an increasing number of our tools and appliances? Or that the sticky, black oil that oozed from the ground in certain regions would fuel vast transportation networks as well as heating our homes and offices, and yielding thousands of different chemicals with hundreds of thousands of industrial uses? We can derive energy from the wind, from sunlight, and even from the bonds that hold chemical elements together. We can send pictures and sound over tiny wires, and even through thin air. There seems to be no limit to what we can fashion out of the stuff of this earth.

Yet each one of us, personally, is acutely aware of limitations. We can only get so much done in a day; our imaginations and desires always outstrip our physical ability to get things done. No matter how much we accomplish, we can always imagine doing more. There is also the problem of all these other people, who frequently get in our way. Sometimes, as with co-workers, they simply don't work fast enough or with sufficient skill. Competitors will often frustrate our aims altogether by claiming the very spaces and materials that we wanted to use.

The biggest obstacle, though, is money. Or, more properly stated, the lack of money. Everything costs money. Each item of physical stuff, whether it is a paper clip or a steel beam, has a price. People, also, require payment—for their labor, their skill, their cooperation. And just as our imaginations can always outpace our ability to deliver the goods, so also our visions can incorporate more costly features than we can afford. Collectively, we have created a world of astounding wonders: huge cities with millions of buildings, networks of roads and communication media that span continents, machines that fly through the air, even craft that journey through space to other planets and beyond. Yet individually, almost without exception, we feel cramped, denied, and prevented from fully spreading our creative wings and displaying all of our magnificent potential to the world. We're convinced, moreover, that the primary factor holding us back is that we simply don't have enough money to properly actualize our dreams.

Try, for a moment, to remove money from the equation. You have energy, you have ability, you have creative vision. The malleable world is all around you. These are the necessary ingredients; money is secondary. Your energy and creativity are associated with doing and being; money is associated with having. You are a being, and you come into this world to do, to engage in certain actions, and to learn and grow through your experience of those actions. Having involves possessing physical material, the stuff of this earth. We are only visitors in this dimension. Each of us is a soul that assumes a body to come here and move things around for a while, and then we take off that garment and withdraw from this world. We are a *being,* not a *having.* When we leave this world, we leave all of our toys behind, for there is no way for us to take those toys, or the sandbox, along with us.

In the free expression of your being, your creativity can run riot. You can build things from scrap materials, compose music, create art, entertain and brighten the lives of everyone around you, all without spending a cent. Have you ever felt so full of your being that you just wanted to go out and embrace the world? The creativity that flows through us comes to us without a price. And we feel best when we do not restrain that flow, but send it out freely into the world.

Each one of us has a varying mix of talents. Through our differing interests and preferences, each will develop an expertise in a wide variety of endeavors. Only in the most primitive of societies, where the members are largely alienated from each other, is total self-subsistence a way of life. Do not confuse self-reliance with self-subsistence. A self-reliant person can be fully integrated into a society of interrelationships where each person contributes what he or she does best to the society at large. In the alienated society of self-subsistence, distrust is the rule, and everyone lives essentially as a hermit.

In the process of building a functioning society, a division of labor arises, in that each person occupies himself with what he does best. Since we all have needs and desires for a wide array of goods and services, the sharing out of the fruits of each person's labors and talents enriches everyone. This is a world of plenty, and our limitless creativity can fashion wonders out of the simplest materials. The potential of human society is for each person to lead a rich, wealthy life. And this view is not for some future date when we have finally figured out how to make the economy function perfectly, this is its inherent condition. It is one that has been achieved countless times over the last several thousand years by tribal societies the world over. Indeed, were it not for the success of our far-flung ancestors, we would not be here in any form. As it is, human societies have survived and thrived for thousands of years, passing down to us a storehouse of riches encompassing literature, philosophy, art, music, sculpture, architecture, medicine, civil codes, domesticated animals, and scientific knowledge. Although some form of money has also been around for thousands of years, it was not the innovation of money that made possible all of the cultural benefits listed above. In fact, most of the advancements that have been bequeathed to us by our distant ancestors were devised *before* money.

Money serves as a medium to facilitate the exchange of dissimilar goods and services, in the same way that an electromagnetic frequency is the medium by which a radio or television program is transmitted from a recording studio into our homes. The frequency is not the program; nor is money, in and of itself, a good or a service. There was wealth before there was money.

The amount of money in the world does not directly determine the amount of affluence or poverty. The more crucial factor is our attitude toward each other. If we believe in scarcity, and that we have to hoard the fruits of the earth before someone else grabs them first, we will seek to cheat, exploit, and impoverish our neighbor. If instead we believe in creative abundance, we will do two things. First, we will seek to express and share out our own creative gifts as widely as possible. In doing so, we will both enrich society and fully realize our own potential. Second, we will wish prosperity upon our neighbors. When all people are thriving and expressing their capabilities to the fullest, there will be a reciprocal distribution of affluence throughout the society.

Material conditions have their roots in our spiritual structure. Poverty stems from distrust, greed, and fear. Affluence is the outgrowth of goodwill, compassion, and a genuine affection for our fellow travelers in this physical realm. Our vibrational emanations seek out compatible frequencies. When we resonate with trust and generosity, abundance will be amplified in our lives.

Chapter Twenty-Two
We Are All Bait

Do you enjoy being singled out, being put on the spot, required to display your talents or mediocrity in a forum where everyone is free to criticize and lambaste you? Probably not. While each one of us has a unique talent to offer the world, and a deep desire to let it shine forth, we also fervently desire that our gift be graciously accepted. Each one of us has a distaste for malicious criticism, and instinctively recoils from harsh rejection. We can all look back upon occasions when we have been embarrassed, and we still shudder at the recollection of rebukes we have suffered, even after decades have passed. Many times, a single humiliating experience will alter the course of our lives, in that it will cause us to abandon an occupation, a course of action, or a dream that was very close to our hearts, and which we felt was the working out of our purpose in this life. Has that ever happened to you? You won't have to think hard about it. For most of us, there are a handful of pivotal experiences, mostly painful, that have caused us to alter our life's course. It may have been rejection by a loved one who we thought would be our mate for life, or betrayal by a business associate that caused us to lose trust in humanity and thus trim back our ambitions for what we might build and produce in this lifetime. Or it may have been nothing more than a cutting remark by a teacher, patron, or odd observer, which occurred at a crucial moment of personal vulnerability, when we were questioning whether we really had the talent to succeed in a certain pursuit. This comment, groundless though it may have been, embarrassed us so profoundly that we turned away from our art, our vocation, or our dream, because we felt that what we were offering was not good enough to be accepted in this world.

First, take hold of this idea: By your very presence in this world, you are good enough to be here. This physical, three-dimensional plane of existence is a very demanding arena in which to live. It requires an enormous sense of adventure and courage to be born into this world, and an immense amount of fortitude to face and navigate all the challenges that come flying at you each day. Beyond that, there's nothing mediocre about the Supreme Being that brought this world and this universe into existence. And you are a portion of that Being. You may not have the greatest singing voice, perhaps you can't dance, and you'll probably never understand quantum physics. You may work in the same uncelebrated job for forty-five years. Still, you are not mediocre. Within you burns the fire of imagination, creation, and love. By engaging your spirit with another person, you have the power to elicit smiles of understanding, laughter, and gratitude. In the most humble yet meaningful way you can infuse comfort, encouragement, and upliftment into each life around you. What could be more divine and special than that?

Of course, it is a fine thing to receive a pep talk that encourages us to display and offer our gifts, whatever they may be. Yet we may still feel reluctant. For we remember with a wince each time that our gifts were not accepted, each stinging, belittling word of criticism. We fear having ourselves and our work treated as bait, to be snipped and bitten at by a horde of unfeeling critics.

But where is this fear coming from? It is originating in our rational mind, which is forever keeping score of our triumphs and defeats. This timid mentality regards every insult and setback as an indelible black mark against us; the rational mind wants everything to be safe, unchanging, and unchallenging forever. We can banish this fear by remembering that we are indestructible. At our core, as possession-less souls, we are unconcerned with ratings, reviews, and win-loss percentages. Whatever we do, we do for the sheer joy of *being*.

It may also be helpful to ponder this notion: In this world, everything is bait. This physical world is in a constant state of dynamic transformation. Every physical thing is engaged in an ongoing process of change. Forms are built up and then they wear away, contributing their material to other forms and transforming into other forms themselves. The most seemingly solid and enduring forms on this planet, the continents, are amalgamations of former continents and sea beds. Vast regions of our present geography, which we now see as solid rock, were worn away from older rocks, grain by grain. Sedimentary rocks, such as shale, sandstone, and limestone, originated from water-borne silts of sand, clay, mud, and seashells. They were deposited in the seas over many millions of years, compressed into new forms of stone by heat and pressure, and eventually thrust up thousands of feet, sometimes to the extent of forming massive mountain ranges like the Alps and the Himalayas. Look at any mountain, and realize that it is bait for the forces of wind and rain. Its lofty reaches will eventually be worn away, grain by grain, until the entire mountain, as sand and silt, has been washed into the sea.

On a much shorter time scale, all living forms reach the end of their physical lives and relinquish their bodies to the processes of decay and transformation. These processes are very much in evidence in a garden. Dead leaves and stems are consumed by earthworms and microorganisms, and turned into new soil components. Even still-living material is not exempt from this process. Caterpillars and other insects, as well as fungi and bacteria, devour green leaves and woody parts of plants, and other insects and animals in turn feed upon them. Many of us are all too aware of being tasty bait for mosquitoes and other biting and sucking insects. Also, many of our diseases stem from the endeavors of viruses, bacteria, and other microorganisms to take over and consume our bodies, even though we are not yet done with them!

It is in the non-physical areas of our lives that we have a harder time reconciling ourselves to this process of tearing apart and recycling. We cherish our work, ideas, and concepts. After all, these are a big part of our gift to the world. And our attitude toward gifts is that we want to see them appreciated. We tend to feel that an integral part of appreciation is preservation. Hence, we find it particularly painful and disturbing when our gifts are not preserved intact but are instead treated as bait, held up in public view for each self-appointed critic to snipe at, dissect, and pick apart.

Forget about the critics. Our function in this world is to live, to express, to experience, to give. The more we let our energy and our talents flow forth, the more we expand our being. If we understand that everything in this world is bait, here to be munched on, consumed, and transformed into something else, we can overcome our fear and reluctance to display and share our gifts. Each day we consume and digest what others have produced, whether it is a pair of shoes, a television program, or a ham sandwich. Some items may last or be remembered longer than others, but eventually everything on this earth will be obliterated as thoroughly as a mountain that has been washed into the sea. We tend to get caught up in the ideas of preservation and permanence. We would do better to acknowledge the transience of all things and instead focus on letting life flow freely.

From the perspective of our soul's development, it is better to be criticized and castigated for offering the fruits of ourselves than it is to withhold our talents and our essence. When we hold back for fear of rejection or ridicule, we are engaging in self-denial of the highest order. For we are trying to deny and suppress our very being. In a sense, we are trying to commit spiritual suicide; we are trying to annihilate ourselves. It's of no use, of course. We're eternal; we can't be snuffed out. If we want to go and sulk in a corner for a month, a year, or a lifetime, that's our prerogative. However, we are only wallowing in pain and discouragement at our own behest, not by the decree of the universe, or of any individual. And, we are delaying our further development and expansion. Also, we are impoverishing others, by denying them our gifts. We have only an incomplete picture of how our offerings are received by others, and of the extended influence and benefit they may convey to people we will never meet. A kind word or act on our part can effect consequences that ripple out beyond our lifetime, to touch and aid people as yet unborn.

While the physical objects we produce will decay and pass away, and even our ideas and laws will be reworked and given new interpretations, the underlying love and goodness we express is indestructible; it will persist in this world, and throughout the universe.

Chapter Twenty-Three
Evil

As part of our mental tendency to set up oppositions, we often use the term evil to define the opposite of good. This word becomes a convenient catch basin into which we throw everything that scares or displeases us. In the daily press and media we see frequent references, by elected officials and average citizens, to evil people, evil nations, and the more amorphous "forces of evil."

This dualistic construct of placing good in opposition to evil is both inaccurate and unfortunate. When we use the word evil, we are in effect excommunicating that person, nation, or thing from any further consideration in our world. We are saying that this person or thing is irredeemably and irrevocably anti-good, no reform or rehabilitation is possible, and this offending party should either be locked away from society forever or destroyed, annihilated, and wiped off the face of the earth.

These are the attitudes of a petulant, spoiled child, one who is under the delusion that he is the sole arbiter of what belongs and does not belong in this world. However, everything belongs here. And everything, whether it manifests any good aspects to us or not, is indelibly imbued with the identity of the Divine.

As creatures who think in dualistic terms, each one of us has been involved in at least one fierce opposition where we have wished that there was some way we could exile or blot out our opponent forever.

This feeling stems from our intense involvement and identification with one side of an issue that has become hotly contested. Since we always see ourselves as the hero, the more intense the division between the opposing sides, the more the other side assumes darker and darker shades of villainy. At such times, while not easy, it is good to take a step back from the heat of the battle and acknowledge that our attitudes and point of view at this moment are exceedingly one-sided.

In cases where someone has committed an especially vicious and depraved crime, there is a tendency to describe the perpetrator as someone who is evil. It takes a little more effort on our part to perceive and understand that this individual is profoundly disturbed and unbalanced. This person may behave in a way that is so dangerous and destructive that for the sake of society's safety he will need to be kept locked away for the rest of his life. But does that person's form of illness or mental derangement constitute evil?

If an animal is severely injured, it will frequently lash out and try to bite anyone who tries to help it. The animal has no intent to injure anyone; it is simply crazed by its own pain. When there is an outbreak of a particularly dangerous and virulent disease, its victims will sometimes be separated, quarantined, from the rest of the population to prevent the spread of the disease. However, we don't classify these people as evil, just sick; once they have recovered their health, they are no longer isolated but return to their normal activities and associations. In the case of a deadly disease, is the infection itself evil? From our point of view, we may consider this disease-producing organism a danger to the survival of our race and worthy of eradication. However, it is simply another form of life going about its business of living, growing, and perpetuating itself.

Imagine that a tribunal of beings from beyond Earth were to convene and judge the innocence or guilt of each species on this planet, based on how they treated all other species. How would humanity fare?

Humans have probably wreaked more injury and destruction upon other life forms than have any other species on this planet. Does that mean we are all evil, and deserve extinction?

We define evil as something that is unalterably opposed to the good, the divine. As such, its fitting fate is to be cast out from the rest of creation, consigned to hell for the rest of forever. This picture may look tidy from a peevish and vindictive point of view. But that's not how reality works. Remember, **everything** is eternal, divine, and united in the One. There is no way to exile or excommunicate anything from the All-There-Is. All is united into Divine Oneness, forever, whether we personally like it or not. All oppositions are ultimately enfolded within the One.

We may take pride in some of our oppositions, feeling that we are the virtuous defenders of the good in a battle with evil villains. It's time to grow up and see that we designate people and things as evil as an excuse for our own hateful feelings, and perhaps dishonest and violent urges. When we look across the divide at our adversaries, we need to realize that they see themselves the same way we see ourselves, as the heroes. Beyond that, we need to take a broader view of the issue which we are contending, and realize that each point of view contains an element of good.

We've discussed earlier how our rational mentality is linear, and therefore unable to simultaneously comprehend all sides or aspects of a thing or situation. We have described the consequent advantages of regarding our dualisms in terms of good and not-good, rather than good versus bad or good versus evil. Creation myths from around the world begin with the fracturing of an original state of unity into pairs of opposing qualities. The opposing qualities are not absolutes in and of themselves, for they are contained within the over-arching reality of All-There-Is. Egyptian creation myth breaks up the unified creation into portions, and places a god over each portion. There are opposing

elements of sky and earth, and a conflict between life and death, represented by Osiris and Set. Although some of the gods are treacherous and
cause destruction from a human perspective, they nonetheless are still
essential features of the whole; and none of them are removed or exiled
from the rest of existence.

In the Hindu myth, the god Shiva has dominion over the forces of
both destruction and renewal. This construct reflects the understanding
that in this physical dimension dead forms are constantly being transformed into new life. Not only do the composting remains of dead organisms sustain new life, so also in our economic activities the buildings
and equipment of defunct companies will be purchased and utilized by
new enterprises.

The notion of evil postulates that there is something-- a consciousness, a force, the devil-- that can stand outside of the All. Not only does
it exist apart from the All, its purpose is to corrupt, degenerate, and destroy the All. The question I've pondered for some time is this: Can any
being or force that is unalterably opposed to good sustain itself? Can
there be a reality in which hate, violence, chaos, and destruction are all
there is?

It is possible for us to conceive of a world and a universe that is good,
and this is usually the image of our universe that we hold in our minds
for most of each day. In this picture of a good world, we love others and
they love us, people cooperate with each other and work for the common good. In essence, a good world is one that works. In a world where
cooperation and kindness prevails, people work together and support
each other, loving relationships flourish, and everything functions. For
the majority of the time, this view is confirmed by the way things actually do work in this world.

What about evil? Can we have a world that is all-evil, where the
devil has won, and all good has been eradicated? What would such a
world look like? First off, each human being would be treacherous and

violent. There would be no one you could trust. Cooperation would not exist; the only relationships would be those in which the strong victimized the weak. Of course, since evil holds sway, murder is rampant; so the human species would soon be reduced to the strongest, most violent individuals. Since no one is loving or trustworthy, we would live solitary, suspicious existences, until we killed each other off. But then, evil is not restricted to humanity alone. Each form of life would be at war with itself and every other life form. And since violence is the order of the day, the elemental forces of the earth and the solar system would also be at war with each other. Planets would collide with one another; the sun would flare out to consume the planets with fire, or suck them from their orbits into its fiery maw. Even this war of the worlds would not carry evil to its fullest expression. In an all-evil universe, there would be no cohesion or cooperation at all, so the atomic bonds that hold all matter together would break apart. Each proton and electron, each quark, photon, and neutrino would be independent and antagonistic to every other particle of matter. Basically, the entire universe would come apart at the seams. All that would remain would be a thin soup of tiny particles, each trying to annihilate all the others.

Sounds ridiculous, doesn't it? My point is that, while a universe based on goodness and cooperation is possible, an all-out, thorough going evil is unsustainable. The idea of a force of evil, by definition, sets up something that is so uncooperative and wracked with conflicts and contradictions that it would annihilate itself the instant it came into existence. It is the tendency of our dualistic way of thinking to split whole things into pairs of opposing qualities. Then we carry these qualities to polar extremes, and imagine these opponents battling each other until one side has been utterly vanquished and destroyed. Such one-dimensional scenarios belong in comic books. They simply aren't applicable to full dimensional reality, where conflicting factors are actually inextricable aspects of the unified whole.

Within this world, and the universe, the forces of heat and cold, growth and decay, expansion and contraction, work together to sustain the whole. The universe is in a perpetual state of unfoldment, and the forces of building up and wearing away are complimentary agents in this pageant of transformation. All of these factors are good, for they are all elements of the whole, the One.

The One encompasses All; it has no opponent. There is no evil to oppose the good. Our conception of evil is a contradiction in terms. It is a figment that has grown out of our flawed, incomplete view of existence; in which we seek to place everything at one extreme pole or its opposite. As I've said before, we think in straight lines, but the universe is curved. When we modify our linear thinking to conform with the curved nature of existence, we will see that the poles that were once far apart and opposite each other will now bend and wrap around until they meet, forming a circle.

Whenever we think of a person, or a group, or thing as evil, we need to look within our own hearts. What is it about this person or group that incites in us feelings of revulsion and rejection that are so strong and intense that we want to exile them, and exclude them from the rest of creation? They have just as much of a valid right to be in this world as we have. Many times our adversaries are only functioning as mirrors to reflect our own unsavory qualities back at us. So what is it *within ourselves* that we are trying to repress or exclude? Every time we feel hostility, it indicates that, in addition to our external opponent, there are inner issues we need to address.

Many times we will regard agents of change as evil, especially if they cause great upheaval and destruction in our lives, like a hurricane or an invading army. However, change and transformation are intrinsic qualities of this world. Sometimes change is mild and gradual; other times it is abrupt and violent. When we react to change by calling the person or force that wrought the change evil, we are attempting to shift the focus away from our fear. We are afraid that we will not be able to cope with the new conditions, the extra work, etc. and so we attempt to deflect attention away from our own feelings of insufficiency by blaming the new state of affairs on something that is beyond the power of a mere mortal—evil. To a great extent, our belief in evil is directly proportional to the amount of fear we have. In order to avoid this trap, realize that you can cope. In one way or another, you will cope. You may not be able to restore everything to the way it was before the upheaval occurred, but you possess the capability and the personal resources to adapt and endure.

We may also assign the designation of evil to someone like a dictator who oppresses and impoverishes the people of his nation. While it may be difficult to summon up any feelings of fellowship or compassion for such an individual, that person, reprehensible as he may be, is not evil. When we regard someone as evil, we are dismissing them, saying that there is no way that we can engage with them in any constructive dialogue or activity. We are admitting our own helplessness and frustration, because we can't figure out how to forge an effective relationship with this person. Just because we are offended, threatened, and frustrated by this person, and they are arrogant, violent, and dishonest, that still does not mean they are evil. Like a villain in a stage play, they are playing a part.

Throughout history, whole societies have enacted dramas and tragedies in which many injustices and atrocities were perpetuated. From the perspective of a single individual caught up in the terror of war or the oppression of tyrants, it may seem that evil indeed holds sway in the world. However, when one is able to survey the scene from the vantage point of unity and eternity, it is possible to see a period of turmoil as a mass endeavor to learn crucial lessons, and to ultimately heal.

By adopting this viewpoint, should one then shrug one's shoulders and turn a blind eye to all the suffering and injustice in the world? Heavens, no. The lessons of humanity, involving kindness, compassion, justice, and a repudiation of violence and exploitation, are issues we are *all* here to deal with, whether we live in a peaceful valley or a war zone. Each one of us, through our actions, thoughts, and emotions, is continuously affecting the state of human society in the entire world. If you want to alleviate suffering and oppression in the world, be kind, generous, honest and understanding with everyone you meet, wherever you are.

When we condemn and label people and things as evil we reduce the sphere of our world, narrow the scope of our mind, and shrink our spirit. We may feel justified in our prejudices and hatreds, because that which we hate is no good at all—it's evil. It takes more inner courage for us to step out from under the shadow of this illusion into the sunshine of the larger world, where there is no such thing as evil, and thus exile and expulsion of those who threaten and offend us is not an option. When we embrace this larger world without evil, we can then expand our awareness and enlarge our capabilities for acceptance, and for expressing love and compassion.

Everything in this world, even that which is difficult and disruptive, has something of value to impart to us. Each one of us represents good in many ways. If we feel that this world is a mean and hostile place, we can only change this situation by expressing more of our own goodness. The more we radiate kindness, goodwill, and acceptance to others, the more we will elicit a reciprocal flow of those qualities from them.

Chapter Twenty-Four
Being Tested, and Encountering New Tests

Some years ago, I saw a wonderful bumper sticker: "Life—This is only a Test." We all too often take ourselves and our lives way too seriously. It is true that what we do here is real, and everything we do produces consequences that ripple out and through the rest of society and the world. Yet this whole earth is a place of learning, experimenting, and trying new things. The whole earth is plastic: in the sense that it is malleable and constantly in a state of flux. Over time, every single thing—from a fly's wing to a marble statue to a vast mountain range—will be transformed and recycled into new forms. Whatever we produce, be it a masterpiece or an utter mess, will eventually decompose and disintegrate, only to be reformed and reintegrated into a new manifestation. Our physical results are nowhere near as important as the attitude with which we undertake and execute our tasks. The vibrations that we project upon this world, whether they are resentment or love, become incorporated into the earth's overall vibrational tone; they have a much more permanent effect on the earth's and humanity's fate than do any of our physical acts.

By regarding each day, and each situation we are confronted with, as a simple test of our capabilities, we can adopt a more lighthearted attitude toward living. For many people, the word *test* may still carry many frightening and threatening connotations. We remember tests in school with a twinge of fear. If we passed, we put that subject behind us and moved on to new topics and endeavors. If we failed, we often had to repeat the same course, and we carried the stigma of *being a failure.* These words resonate like doom; it's as if a permanent black mark has been smudged upon our soul. But let's demolish this delusion right here and now. You are a being. You may succeed at certain things, and fail at others. But success and failure are not, and never will be, intrinsic attributes of your being. **Your soul is beyond success and failure.** Your soul simply is. When you incarnate on the Earth plane, you come here to live. In the process of living and acting, certain things you attempt to do will turn out as you planned, and other things will not. Many times, however, it is on those occasions when things do not turn out as you planned that you reap the greatest benefits. You have heard other people say, and you have probably said so several times yourself, that when a project did not succeed, it was actually a blessing in disguise. When things go awry and don't turn out as planned, we often learn valuable information and are presented with new acquaintances and opportunities that otherwise would not have come our way.

One time, at an auction, I purchased an entire room full of goods as a single lot. My initial elation quickly turned to dismay when I discovered that most of the goods were useless, and that it was going to cost me more money—considerably more—to have all this worthless material carted away and junked. What I had envisioned as a straightforward, lucrative enterprise had become an intricate series of negotiations and financially precarious arrangements. At every step along the way, I didn't know what I was doing; it was luck, rather than business savvy, that kept me from losing my shirt. At the end of the experience, when I had finally disposed of everything, I had a good laugh. I had not achieved my objective of scoring a great financial success. Yet I had received a tremendous education in a field that previously I had known nothing about. My imagination, resourcefulness, and perseverance were tested in ways that could not be gauged in terms of a monetary profit or loss. I realized that tests are not about passing or failing. Rather, they are situations that fully engage our entire person and force us to *live*.

Let's go back to the original vision of failure that haunted virtually every one of us when we were in school: that of failing a subject. Say you did fail a subject, and had to repeat it. By taking the course a second time, you were able to grasp and understand what you missed the first time around, so that you gained from the experience. Also, most likely, you were exposed to a different teacher and classmates. You may have made new friends or met people who would have a significant influence on the rest of your school career. You may have initially failed the course because you were inattentive and neglected to study. Retaking the course may have stimulated you to become more serious about school and to develop good study habits, from which you have benefited ever since. Sometimes it takes a failure or setback to shock us into reordering our priorities, so that we become more organized and effective in everything we do from then on.

The dread and fear of failure hangs over many people like a dark cloud that casts a shadow over their attitudes and belief in themselves. However, determining success or failure is a very subjective thing. Let's consider a couple of sports. How do you define success, as opposed to failure, in golf? Is it shooting par for the course? Professional golfers often score below par, while most casual golfers never come within ten strokes of that mark. So what is success at golf? Or how about bowling? Here, there is a definite perfect score, 300, but few people ever roll such a game. Are they all failures? Perhaps the successful player is the person who has fun while playing these games. After all, sports are activities that were devised for the sheer enjoyment of the event.

Understand that in the larger context or existence, there is neither winning nor losing, succeeding or failing—there is only being. When we participate in a specific contest, we give it our best effort, but we don't always win the prize. According to our accounting mentality, we have lost. But when we take the larger view, we will see that by engaging in the contest, we have lived. And that's why we came into the material plane. Not to cross each finish line first, but to know the thrill, the effort, the pain, and the exhilaration of participating in the race. Imagine a play in which two characters are adversaries. Over the course of the play they struggle against each other, and in the end one character prevails, and the other is vanquished. The same two actors perform in this play hundreds of times. Each night the same actor wins, while the other actor loses. Would you say that the actor who loses every night is a failure? Of course not; he's just pretending to be a certain character in a play. He takes on a role and plays it for all he is worth. In fact, by persuading each night's audience to believe in his character's utter defeat, he is succeeding splendidly—as an actor.

In the same way, the body you presently inhabit, which may not be particularly dashing or athletic, is not *you*. Nor is the personality you presently inhabit, which pleases some people and irritates others. These are elements of the role you are presently playing. And like the actor in the play, the successes and failures you experience on the stage of this world are not intrinsic to yourself, they are simply roles you acted out.

So, life is only a test. Failing a test is only an intermediate position on your way to passing it. The key is to maintain an attitude of adventure and take joy in the journey. Passing and failing are merely different varieties of experience that you come to this world to sample. Your soul is beyond the dimension of categorization. You are neither a success nor a failure; neither hero nor villain. You simply are.

Once we become familiar with this concept that life is only a test, there is one little related matter to consider. As long as you are in this world, you are going to be tested. Just as all physical matter is involved in a continuous transformation into new forms, so too your spirit will continually be presented with new opportunities and challenges. As soon as you have mastered one skill, or think you now understand life and will never be upset or disturbed again, a new, unimagined test will tap you on the shoulder, or, more likely, pull the rug out from under your feet.

This world is inexhaustible. As a human being, you will never master every aspect and feature of it. Since you are here to learn and grow, once you attain a certain level of mastery, there will always be new lessons to challenge you to ascend to the next level. It is a common feature of our rational minds to think that once we have solved our present crisis, we will be in the clear. No other situation or battle will be able to perturb us as much as the one we are currently engaged in, so after this mess is out of the way, the rest of our life will be clear sailing. The rational mind magnifies whatever it is currently thinking about and shrinks everything else, so that the challenge of the present moment always seems to be the biggest, most dangerous, and most important one we will ever face.

There is a phrase that politicians, advertisers, and commentators, as well as you and your neighbors, use all the time: "Now more than ever..." As if there was never any moment in the earth's history more fraught with necessity and peril than the present one. Understand that, many times in your life, perhaps weekly, you will be facing a pivotal situation. The present one may be more crucial than the situation you dealt with last week, or it might only seem so. It's not that the situations you're confronting now are becoming ever more dangerous with each passing day. What is happening is that **the pivot points keep changing.** As you solve issues in one area of your life, other aspects will come to the fore and offer you the opportunity to master them. The pivotal situation you are facing now is different from the ones you have resolved in the past.

Imagine cranes erecting the steel frame of a skyscraper. When the structure is twenty stories high, the cranes are at the twenty-story level.

As the girders are raised and bolted and welded into place, the cranes are jacked up, floor by floor. A month or so from now, the steel structure is thirty-five stories high, and the cranes are at that level. Soon they will be fifty stories up; then sixty, then seventy. As one level is completed, they rise to the next. When the cranes are on the forty-second floor, the crane operators focus on the work that needs to be done on that floor. Whatever challenges they may have faced on the twenty-third or thirty-seventh floors are now of little importance. They are rightly concerned with the immediate situation.

As we live from day to day, there will always be compelling issues for us to face. Some may be more physically threatening, irritating, or may require more effort to resolve than do others. But there will always be a new test for us to face. Realize that with each new test, you are improving and refining your skills for living in this physical dimension. You are also, as it were, getting your money's worth out of this life. Keep remembering that you are eternal and indestructible. Each test you face is like a new dance partner inviting you to take a spin around the gleaming dance floor of this earth, and with each partner you will learn new steps and movements you didn't know you were capable of executing. The dance of life offers endless variations. Immerse yourself in them and enjoy the full variety of life.

Chapter Twenty-Five
Unconditional Love

We have noted that our emotions correspond to specific vibratory frequencies. You resonate at a certain frequency when you are happy, and at an altogether different frequency when you are angry. While romantic attraction and affection also have distinct vibratory signatures, the larger quality, which we simply term love, seems to be in a class by itself. Certain frequencies correspond to various aspects of the overall emotion we call love, yet none of them, nor all of them together, can fully pin down or define everything that we are feeling and expressing.

There are aspects of love that go beyond all the frequencies that we can associate with our emotions. You might say that love is the fundamental emanation of the All-There-Is. I personally suspect that, if science ever does manage to formulate a grand Theory of Everything that incorporates all the forces and properties of the universe, the underlying factor that holds the whole thing together will be love.

The basis of every story in the entire world is love. In a story with a positive outcome, love triumphs. Where love is withheld or denied, relationships falter, conflict arises, and tragedy ensues.

Love is central to our lives. All of our dreams for our personal future, and the ideal society in which we want to live, feature cooperation, peace, goodwill, abundance, happiness, and radiant health. The bedrock upon which these qualities, and the catalog of everything else we consider desirable rest, is love.

Therefore, in the lives we picture for ourselves, which we work toward manifesting each day, we seek to surround ourselves with love. Our ideal world would be one in which the network of all of our connections to other people, and the larger world, would form a nurturing cocoon of loving relationships all around us. This is a universal desire, and while there are some individuals among us who are diseased and unbalanced to such a degree that they inflict harm and pain upon those around them, even here, without love, they would not survive at all. Love creates cohesion. From the tiniest specks of life on this planet to the largest and most sophisticated organisms, cohesion is essential for life. At the microscopic level, if molecules will not adhere together, if the loving bond of trust and cooperation cannot be made between the chemical elements, then life cannot exist.

We all need love, and it is a common trait of humanity that we are concerned with having our needs met. In this case, it means that we usually think first about receiving love. In the rational sense, this seems pretty logical. Once our needs are met, we will then feel secure and safe enough to return love to others, to be supportive, compassionate, and kind. But first, we need to look out for number one. However, treated in this way, love can be a funny thing. When we treat it as a good to be exchanged, bought with favors, hoarded and kept away from those who are unworthy, and twisted into a thousand grotesque counterfeits of what it really is, love vanishes. We end up with relationships by contract, instead of mutual affection and trust.

Love is free. It pervades the universe. And it is inexhaustible. You can never use it all up or run out of it. If you really want to be a loving person, you must be like the sun. The sun radiates its light and energy in all directions. It doesn't withhold its essence. It blazes forth for all it is worth. The sun doesn't play favorites, such as sending more energy to the Earth because we humans are so wonderful, or shading out Saturn because it's such a heavy, dour planet.

As physical beings who can only pursue one activity at a time, we will of course discriminate according to our tastes, and have certain items and people we prefer over others. Yet it is within our capacity to send out love to everything and everyone we encounter. It is also a towering challenge, for we have spent our whole lives up to this point splitting the world into opposing categories of likes and dislikes. We are not alone, for this is the primary thrust of rational human society. This attitude is promulgated and reinforced by every organization and grouping of people. It is, however, an unfortunate practice, for it leads us to a lot of separation and conflict.

While we all have love in our hearts, most of us express our love conditionally. You know how this scene works: "I'll love you *if* you love me." Inside, we're yearning to express our love, yet we have been conditioned by society to feel like a fool if we unreservedly express our love and not receive any love in return. Our rational mind tells us that there has to be some form of fair exchange: love given must be matched by love received. This kind of setup may work okay when it comes to exchanging goods in a marketplace, but it is completely out of place in the realm of love. As St. Paul puts it in a Biblical passage that is frequently quoted during wedding ceremonies, "Love seeks not after itself." What does this mean? It means that love has no self-interest. It does not seek to receive or possess anything. Love can stand alone; it doesn't need any reciprocal arrangement to prop it up.

Like the sun beaming without restraint in all directions, love is unconditional. There is an old saying that Love is blind. This phrase does not mean that we are oblivious and unaware of another person's foibles and faults. Rather, love permits us to see beyond the temporal garment of imperfections and differences that we all wear in this physical dimension. With this blind love, our perception transcends the boundaries and qualifications that have been erected by petty rationality, and we receive a glimpse of the underlying unity we all share, where each one of us is an intrinsically wonderful and love-able entity.

To know true love, we must love without reservation, without any conditions. So many times we will love someone or something as long as it is cooperative, convenient, and pleasing to us. Unconditional love means loving a person even when he or she is at his most recalcitrant, obnoxious, and displeasing. It means loving persons and things that society usually conditions us to dislike. This is a tall order, but it is not insurmountable. To learn how to love in this manner, it is helpful to start with someone or something you already like. There are rough patches in every friendship and relationship, and it is precisely in these difficult intervals that you can develop the skills to love unconditionally. Practice sending love to this person continuously: no matter what he says or does, no matter how she treats you. Let your love flow forth like a river, which is ceaselessly pouring itself into the sea.

Think for a moment of the traditional wedding vows, in which the bride and groom promise to love each other, "for better or for worse, for richer or for poorer, in sickness and in health." What are they promising? That they will love each other *regardless of the conditions* the future may bring. This is the essence of unconditional love: My love is unwavering; it will not be affected, augmented, or diminished by any conditions we may encounter. My love for you is an eternal, indestructible thing that exists outside of all the temporal circumstances and conditions of this world.

Pretty heady stuff, huh? This is the love for which each one of us yearns, and which it is within our capacity to extend to others. When we transcend the conditions with which we so often restrict the flow of love, we will also begin to transcend the ego-pettiness that so frequently feels offended, insulted, and slighted—and that instigates alienation and enmity.

What is this ego, and why does it cause us so much grief? The ego is our sense of self as an entity with interests to pursue in this world. It is aligned with, although not exactly the same as, our personality. The ego has a constructive purpose: it instills us with self-confidence and self-es-teem. In this respect, the ego is our personal motivator and cheering section, urging us to fulfill our life's purpose, and shouting constantly, "You can do it! You can do it!"

Problems arise when the ego focuses too intently on the I-alone, to the point where building self-confidence crosses over into the territory of self-importance and arrogance. If we allow ourselves to move in this direction, the ego will then formulate a set of expectations for how we should be treated, recognized, and acknowledged. When people do not treat us in a way that measures up to these standards, the ego is offended.

You know what happens when you feel hurt and offended—you take out your revenge on the offending party by refusing to cooperate with them, or by withdrawing your friendship and affection. When the ego's conditions are not met, its only tactic is to retaliate by offending the conditions of other people's egos. It's good to keep in mind that all the other people also have egos that are doing their utmost to bolster their self-esteem. And they are just as susceptible to feeling hurt, offended, and vengeful as we are.

Looked at in this way, it's pretty obvious that *the ego is not us.* It is more like a universal tool that each one of us employs for self-motiva-tional purposes. All tools have a limited range of application. A hammer is a great tool for driving nails, but hopelessly ineffective for removing screws. Likewise, the ego has a limited range of applicability. It works well to bolster our sense of individual competence and self-worth. But it does us a disservice when it conjures up a list of self-gratifying condi-tions, stipulating that we withhold our essence and retreat from society if those conditions are not met.

We take a great stride in the direction of asserting our independent spirits when we take charge of our actions and responses, instead of re-acting reflexively to situations the ego has labeled offensive and unac-ceptable. When it comes to unconditional love, it is necessary to step outside of the framework of conditions that the ego has constructed, and to understand that this framework is an artificial structure that has been hemming in our limitless spirit. Even armed with this understanding, dissolving this edifice of conditions will be a monumental endeavor for most of us. For the ego will not give up without a fight. It rather likes feeling offended, because every perceived slight gives it another chance to build up its self-esteem while at the same time denigrating the value of others. The ego is very much a creature of the rational faculty; because it is intimately tied to rational thinking, it deals wholeheartedly in dualities. It excels at setting up oppositions. However, *the ego is not us;* it is a tool. Just as any one of a million people can pick up a shovel and use it to dig a trench, so too we all use the faculty of ego in the same standard ways. We can go one step further, and consider that the rational faculty is not us, either. Just like the ego, it is a common tool that humanity employs, in much the same way that we use our legs to walk and our hands to grasp things.

True love transcends the arena of duality and contending agendas. When we love unconditionally, there is no opposition, no right or left, no east or west. Like the sun, our love radiates out in all directions. In the case of loving someone unconditionally, our love is extended to that person regardless of the emotion he or she may be projecting toward us—acceptance or rejection, affection or hostility, respect or disdain. While the ego cares about how we are treated, the unconditionally loving self does not. We have historical accounts of saintly people who have loved their detractors and oppressors without reservation. They have even loved their executioners.

There is a quality which serves as a stepping-stone to unconditional love. That is humility. An ego-driven sense of self-importance confines a person to dealing only with those people and situations that meet the ego's conditions and expectations. According to these terms, many people, ideas, and activities will be beneath one's consideration. Hence, this person has sharply curtailed his own freedom. In contrast, the humble person realizes that the ego is a simple tool and uses it for appropriate purposes without allowing it to inflate to detrimental proportions. Thus, this person remains free to engage in all sorts of endeavors and associate with all people.

With humility, we are open to perceiving beauty in the most unlikely places and to recognizing the value in the most derelict of human beings. The humble person knows, deeply, that everything has considerable value. He remains aware that we are all divine beings, and hence much more than we appear to be in our human disguises. Each time we encounter another person, no matter how well or poorly they are dressed, whether they smell of perfume or stink of vomit, be they highly educated or mentally handicapped, beautiful or ugly, we are encountering another aspect of the divine. Just as we have come here with a certain agenda and a specified role to play, every other person is also fully engaged in performing a role—one that he assigned himself to proceed with his personal development. It is not for us to judge the value of someone else's assignment. The life of a social misfit may have no appeal to us. But, for the person living it, that life experience contains a compelling and powerful lesson that he or she feels is essential to learn.

Humility allows us to encounter each person at his own level, and to apprehend the whole world on its own terms. When we do so, we will feel genuine kinship with each person and thing, and an outpouring of love will be our spontaneous response. This love, unshackled from all conditions, will dissolve the boundaries that separate us from one another. The more purely we can express our love, the closer we will come to understanding and experiencing the Unity of all Reality.

Chapter Twenty-Six
Acknowledging One's Worthiness

Have you sometimes had a clear realization of a spiritual truth, in which you could see a better way of acting and relating than the way you're living right now? Have you been seized with a sense of excitement as you perceive all the positive changes that could occur almost spontaneously if you were to begin acting in accordance with this truth? Have you felt a surge of energy welling up from deep within you, producing a flush of confidence throughout your body, with the words pulsing in your brain: "You can do it!" Have you ever felt this way?

What has happened next? Have you acted on this magnificent impulse, or has a sudden backlash of fear swept over your enthusiasm and confidence, submerging them under a chattering tide of "You can't! You can't!" I'm sure you've heard the litany many times. You can't because: so-and-so will disapprove; you're not smart enough, strong enough, rich enough, brave enough, and so forth. Right here, let's go back to a fundamental truth. Your soul is whole and complete. **By the very fact of your existence, you are enough.** So, now what's stopping you?

Each one of us has many fine impulses that we shy away from expressing because we feel that they are not sanctioned by society. Or because freely expressing kindness and generosity will be seen as a sign of weakness, and we will be cheated, ridiculed, and taken advantage of until all our material resources are gone. The prevailing attitude, which is broadcast incessantly by the media and voiced each day by almost everyone, is that the world is a hard and nasty place, and you must be suspicious of everyone. Well, who made this awful society that we're stuck in? Was it some evil genius, or a conspiracy of greedy and powerful individuals? No. This society, for better or worse, is the product of you, me, and every one of us. It is what it is because that is what we make it each day. It doesn't have to be so tough and brutal. All we have to do is lighten up and stop being so tough and brutal to one another.

Are you ready to start? Or are you going to wait until someone is nice to you first? If you take a step back from the world and look at the situation, it seems almost absurd. Here are all these human beings, individuated sparks of the Divine Fire, wanting to love, wanting to be loved, yet feeling vulnerable and insecure, and thus waiting for someone else to make the first move. To make this a better world, we all need to plunge in, with all our vulnerabilities in full view, and offer our best. Be giving, loving, kind, and compassionate.

Many times throughout our lives we do plunge in. Every time we give someone the benefit of the doubt, forgive an injury or insult, or initiate a loving contact with another person, we are overcoming our fears and endeavoring to raise the condition of the whole of humanity, Remember, we are all linked together on one vast human wavelength, and the vibration of humanity is fed and affected by each one of us. Each one of us, through our emotions and deeds, nudges this vibration a little higher or lower. In the conduct of your affairs each day, which way are you moving this vibration?

It may be helpful to remember, as you are teetering on the brink of plunging in with your love or retreating into your fear, that you are invulnerable. Yes, as a human being you can feel physical pain and emotional hurts. But your underlying, intrinsic nature is eternal and indestructible. You come to this plane of existence to confront fears and see just how fully you can overcome them. No matter what happens here, whether you are cheated, abused, embarrassed, or humiliated, you are going to come out on the other side of these experiences. Fully intact. Remember, it's only a test. In fact, better than using the word *test,* consider this life and its challenges as an *exercise.* Similar to working out to develop your muscles, each situation in your life—each problem, challenge, potential relationship—is simply an exercise to see how fully you can respond in a loving and constructive way.

We all have a self-image that we carry in our minds of how we really are, and how we would like others to see us. In your mind's eye, who are you? What are those qualities that are always in your heart, the foundation upon which your character is built? If the world could see the real you, as you see yourself, what would they see? A person brimming with interests and love, eager to bask in the glow of friendship; cooperative, supportive, inquisitive, fond of laughter, desirous of respect, fun to be with? An all around, thoroughgoing good person, yes? Take a moment to turn within and gaze upon this marvelous being which is yourself. If there is a disconnect between this wonderful person you know you are, and your outer manifestation, what is in the way? You can say it's your job, your family, an antagonistic neighbor, the economy; but these are all externalities. What is *within you* that is obstructing the flow of your loving energy, enthusiasm, and talent?

Perhaps you may feel that you are simply too weak, flawed, and mediocre to be a glowing, inspiring presence in this world. But that's nonsense. Even if you have known only one or two such moments in your life, there have been times when you have glowed and dazzled, when you were the spark that ignited exhilaration and happiness in others. Remember those moments when you were a star, and just like a celestial star, you let the magnificence of your being radiate unimpeded out in all directions. Those occasions were not rare moments of grace when you were given a glimpse of a state you might attain in some future life, they were revelations of your true inner state, as it exists right now. All you have to do to recapture that state is to clear away the clutter of fears, disappointments, and negative memories.

How do you feel about Bhudda, Moses, Jesus, Mohammed, and all the other great adepts, teachers, and saints of human history? Are they special entities, who just happened to drop in here on Earth to give the rest of us wayward souls the gift of their good example? Were they really so much different, or better, than you and me? Accounts of their lives show that, while they did and said many inspiring things, they were far from perfect. Many were libertines, thieves, and oppressors before they confronted and cleared away their own inner conflicts and turmoil. In each case, they were born into this world just like you and me: naked, hungry, and vulnerable to the same pains and ills that afflict us. Is there any distinguishing difference between them and us? Only that they took the plunge. They cast off their fears and expressed their true inner selves without reservation.

Now, what about you? Are you as good, wonderful, and holy a person as Mahatma Ghandi, Martin Luther King, or Mother Theresa? Forget the false modesty, the crutch of unworthiness that you have used all your life to avoid really being put on the line. Can you see yourself as a person who is, in every respect, equal to Jesus Christ? You may have been instructed that it is blasphemy and the sin of pride to place yourself on the same level as one of such exalted goodness. But here is my point: Until you see yourself as being the equal of Jesus Christ, **and start acting like it,** this world, and human society, will be in sorry shape.

You, me, Mohammed, Bhudda, and Jesus are all equally endowed with the spark of divinity. Some of us may express the purity of that love and wisdom more strongly than do others. But down deep, at the soul level, we are all equals. And each one of us has the same potential to manifest that radiance in this world.

Many people will shy away from this concept. Some will be highly offended. Essentially, they will protest that they are much too flawed, imperfect, and sinful to be placed on a par with the great saints and spiritual teachers of history. But what are they actually saying? "I'm flawed and sinful, and I intend to stay that way!" By owning up to our true divine nature, we lose all of our excuses for our petty, irritable, and deceitful behavior.

You are a god. Are you prepared to start living and acting like one? Ponder these questions for a while, and realize that you can ascend to levels of saintliness, or descend to levels of exploitation and depravity. The choice is yours. Realize that you haven't been seduced or forced into acting the way that you presently do. Whether you want to admit it or not, the way you are right now is the result of the choices you have made. If the reflection you see in the mirror is not the wonderful person you believe deep down you are, and if that reflection looks like a crook or a tyrant compared with Ghandi or St. Francis, go back over your choices.

When you clearly understand that you are a wondrous child of the All-One, and thus immediate kin to every great and holy person who has ever existed, you will then realize that, if you do not presently exemplify all of their saintly traits, it is because you have chosen to live otherwise. You can't blame your parents, your employer, your spouse, your neighbors, the economy, the government, the weather, or the world situation.

You are as holy, as good, as closely connected to the Supreme Being as Jesus Christ. True, we all have different strengths and abilities. Some people are natural musicians, some have great mechanical aptitude, some are born into wealthy families with extensive financial resources at their disposal. And we all encounter varying degrees of suffering, illness, deprivation, oppression, and the like. Still, the Divine spark is forever within us. Whether we are clothed in formal attire or tattered rags, rich or poor, physically perfect or horribly deformed, we are still capable of blazing forth like the sun with love and kindness. The various pains and sufferings we have endured may be handicaps, hurdles placed in our path, but they are not excuses for beastly behavior. They are only challenges. Tests—no, exercises—to stimulate us to flex and develop the muscles of our love and compassion. We are, each one of us, saints and angels. At times, with our petty moods, resentments, and enmities we can disguise our true god-natures, like children wearing Halloween costumes. However, beneath the grotesque costumes, we are still divinely-endowed, wondrous beings.

Some of the ideas in the above paragraphs may be a little challenging or startling to you, but it is nothing new. These concepts have been recorded in spiritual traditions going back thousands of years. It is simultaneously exciting and frightening. It is exciting to consider that you have the capability, during this lifetime, to attain a full spiritual realization of your Divine nature while you are on this physical plane. And in that fully realized state, you will be an irresistible force for healing and peace and cooperation in the world. Yet it is also a little unsettling when you consider that every other person, in your town and the world, possesses the same potential. A series of trivial doubts and fears may spring to your mind. How can your neighbor be just as divine as you are? Everyone knows you are a much nicer and generous person. Also, if every person suddenly became saintly and radiant, how would the economy function? Who would do all the dirty grunt work?

This dilemma has bedeviled people throughout the ages. For while each one of us seeks liberation for ourselves, and may wish to transcend the negative, limiting patterns of thinking and acting that cause us to plod through day after day, we fear a transformation that would overturn the entire status quo. Again, our fears get the better of us, and frighten us into thinking that we might not like or be able to cope with an entirely changed society. For these reasons, many spiritual truths, while they have been known for thousands of years, have often been concealed from the general public, restricted to priesthoods and other secret societies.

It's a funny thing about secrets. The world, as we have presently constructed it, is full of secrets. There are secret clubs, government secrets, trade secrets, secret ingredients, and dirty little secrets that we're all trying to keep from one another. Now, as we learned earlier, the truth always outs, so there really are no secrets. Or, at least, if someone wants to discern a particular piece of information that one or several other people are trying to prevent him from learning, he will be able to do so, because the truth is an independent vibration, accessible to everyone. And yet, many facts are locked away even though they can be discerned. None of us has the time or inclination to attempt to reveal all that has been concealed. Still, the whole idea of keeping secrets from one another needs to be explored. Fear is the motivating force behind secrets. Fear of possible aggression from other nations will cause a country to keep the details of its own defenses and weapons secret. A company, fearing competition, will lock away its recipes and the procedure manuals for its industrial processes. Our own fear of revealing the truth behind our motives and actions will lead us to keep secrets from our friends, relatives, and neighbors. There is still a greater fear, that of upsetting the status quo, that leads us to conceal our understanding of how the world works, and the spiritual truths of how we can live joyous, enlightened lives.

However, one factor that really impressed itself on me is that, if some of us do reincarnate into this world, we may operate for one or many lifetimes under the handicap of having certain essential knowledge withheld from us. I don't know about you, but in this lifetime I have worked hard to learn and uncover certain spiritual truths. If I'm going to come back here in another life and start out as a child again, I don't want to have to spend years rediscovering all the spiritual precepts that it took me so long to unearth in this lifetime. I want them to be out in the open, part of everyone's elementary education, so that I can move on and explore deeper and more profound issues. Therefore, I don't want the spiritual insights I now possess to be locked away by any priesthood or secret society. And neither should you. If you have a great insight or discovery, let it be widely known. By sharing it out openly, you will bring benefits to many people. And one of those people may be yourself, in your next life.

Also, there is the issue of holding back, either by trying to conceal the knowledge and talent you have, or by thinking that you need to conserve your energies and abilities, lest you exhaust your talent and end up impoverished, with nothing of value left to give. One of the essential features of your being is that you are inexhaustible. You have a direct line into an infinite well of energy, creativity, and talent. If anything, the more you give of yourself, the more you open up this channel, so that you will have even more to give. Keep in mind that you didn't come here just to produce a pristine, unused corpse at the time of your death. You came here to live, to stir things up, to dance, to love, to learn, to fill your fists with material reality and intimately find out what it is all about. It's your ride; make sure you get your money's worth. Give as much of yourself as you can, for there is always more of you than the world can hold. Make full use of your talents and the time of your life. They are here to be used—you can't cash them in for a refund when you're leaving this world.

It is time to put our fears aside. First off, let's stop preventing ourselves and each other from creating a society of fully realized, exuberant, saintly beings. When each person is living in the joy of fully expressing his love and creativity, we will be living in a truly olden age. And all the work will get done, at least all the services necessary for a functioning society. It is true that a number of occupations, those focused primarily on contention and opposition, may not be as prominent or necessary as they are today. As for the so-called dirty jobs, they will be done with relish. In our present society we typically look down on manual labor and the humble household chores of daily life. We have sold ourselves on the idea that we have to be important, and we have attached importance to having power, giving orders, making deals, and making lots of money. Most of us today have lost sight of the great value of simple manual tasks. Remember that physicality is not our normal state. We are spiritual beings. Even though at times this life may seem to be long, stultifying, and boring, it is actually a brief visit to the material realm, and a profound opportunity to gain concrete experience with matter. Most of us, ironically, spend most of our lives avoiding physical tasks; we have invented machines; and air conditioning keeps us from sweating.

However, if you can find a master craftsman, someone who works with his hands, you will commonly find that he is engaged in a lifelong love affair with his craft. He will never be able to exhaust all the nuances of his work, nor penetrate all the mysteries of how his movements and the material he is working with interact.

In each simple deed and task, there is a wealth of deep connection and relationship with the physical matter we are working with. In eastern philosophy, an instruction for attaining enduring enlightenment states simply, "Chop wood, carry water." The humble tasks are deceptively mundane. Each speck of matter contains more meaning and potential revelation than all the libraries on Earth. Our sense of self-importance, of being above certain humble chores, seals off access to this realm of meaning and intimate relationship.

Little children derive the greatest fascination and pleasure from the simplest materials. Observe a toddler celebrating her first Christmas. She may be surrounded by dozens of shiny, blinking toys. Yet what does she find endlessly interesting and intriguing? The wrapping paper. Because the child is not caught up in assigning rational valuations to all objects, she has the freedom to apprehend the whole world on its own, meaning-laden terms. So the child is easily amused and becomes engaged with every object within her reach. Not because she is too ignorant to ascertain what is valuable and what is not. Rather, she is still capable of perceiving the true value intrinsic in every thing. There is also intrinsic value residing in every activity, from sweeping a floor or preparing a meal to designing a computer or performing surgery.

In the money economy, we have devalued commonplace, manual activities and exalted those that require the most technical expertise, or those performed by people who occupy select positions at the apex of concentrations of great wealth, such as investment bankers. The unfortunate outcome of this process is that we have, by extension, devalued all the persons who perform humble tasks, such as cooking, cleaning, and nurturing young children and the sick. The irony is that human societies have survived and prospered for thousands of years without investment bankers; if we were to cease nurturing the young, however, humanity would collapse in a generation.

This attitude of glorifying ostentatious wealth and brash dealmakers while devaluing manual labor gushes from the print and electronic media every day. It creates and perpetuates a consciousness of inferiority and envy. If we subscribe to such a mentality, our awareness will be consumed with concerns about getting and spending, and we will lose touch with the realms of meaning that are right at our fingertips.

However, those realms of meaning are still accessible to us. All we have to do is set aside our envious, acquisitive mentality. Recall a recent day when you had some time off. You may have taken an excursion to a beach or a park, or even spent time at home sorting through some stuff. At some point you were totally undirected, just idly shaping sand on a beach, fingering a smooth stone that caught your attention, or rearranging odd items in a desk drawer. For a moment there was just you and the material you were touching. Your motions were simple, inconsequential, yet strangely and immensely comforting and satisfying. When we humbly connect with the material world, and acknowledge the value in every action and thing, we can enter into and sustain a state of joy and fulfillment while we work.

Can you imagine a society in which you and every other person loved their work, felt appreciated, and eagerly anticipated each new day? This scenario is not some pie in the sky fantasy. It is our birthright, and all the required materials are right at our fingertips. The only adjustment we have to make is to our attitudes regarding work and value; we have to become willing to relinquish our fears and unchain our inner enthusiasm and unconditional love. Somebody's got to start this process. Be brave. Be exuberant. Take the plunge. Remember, you're indestructible, and you're here for the adventure of this life.

Start by looking at the fears you have regarding your own transformation. While many of us are afflicted with a fear of failure, just as often we hold ourselves back because of our fear of success. It may sound preposterous for anyone to be afraid of success, but look back at the times that you have turned away from promising opportunities. Success usually brings changes, and sometimes we will cling to the rut we are in, uncomfortable though it may be, because we are at least accustomed to it. Changes may well involve new responsibilities, and again our fear of being equal to the task will hold us back. Remember that you have the same direct connection to all the abilities and talents that other people have tapped into. You are able. You are sufficient. You are worthy. You are a Divine being. Each day, with each thought and deed, let your divinity shine through. You will be astounded at the transformations you can bring about in yourself, and in the world around you.

Chapter Twenty-Seven
The Empty Soul

While we are engaged in living in this world, we are fully involved with the physical body we inhabit. In the thinking terms that are also an intrinsic feature of our consciousness in this world, whenever we think of who we are, we see the picture of our face and body. Even when we may ponder the afterlife we see ourselves as our present physical representation, or at least an idealized (slimmer, trimmer) form of it. When we think of reuniting with departed friends and relatives, we again imagine them with the physical features they had when we last saw them in this world. After all, how else will we know them?

This intense identification with the garment of our bodies is entirely understandable. Yet, to penetrate beneath the surface aspects of this world, so that we can more fully understand the nature of who we are, within and beyond it, we must cultivate a more detached view. We are not our bodies, just as we are not the clothes we put on this morning. We are going to delve a little into the nature of the soul, so flex the muscles of your imagination.

I will use the term *soul* to refer to the non-material being that each one of us is. Whether we use the word *spirit, soul,* or *being,* the individuated consciousness we are referring to is something that has no mass, no structure, no traits whatsoever. In the context of this world, we think most of the time in terms of *having.* We have a body, clothes, car, house, furnishings, and so forth. We identify ourselves with these things, such as, "I have a pain in *my* shoulder," or, "I *own* a house at the beach." As we go through life we keep gathering possessions, both physical and non-physical, such as memberships in various groups and associations. We use all of these things we have accumulated as markers to identify who we are, so that we are the owner of a piece of real estate, an alumnus of that school, a member of that country club, a contributor to this charity, and such. Also, we tend to believe, in general, that the more possessions we have amassed, the bigger a person we are: more important, more esteemed, more realized and fulfilled. Yet, all of these material possessions, plus our degrees, titles, memberships, and associations, are all just the stuff of this world. We possessed none of it before we entered this world, and we will relinquish all of it when we leave. Understand that *having,* possessing things, is a quality of this world. But there are no corresponding qualities of ownership or possession in spiritual dimensions.

With a little exercise of your imagination you can begin to picture a realm where clothes, cars, houses, food, and all other material objects are not essential. Now, let's strip away some of the deeper qualities that you consider to be a part of your intrinsic character, such as your intelligence, courage, loyalty, short temper, sense of humor. Let's remove all of your virtues and vices. And also your name. While you are totally attached to it right now, your name is a small item; you only acquired it when you acquired your present body. There is another thing that you probably feel existed before this lifetime, and as a part of the intrinsic you will persist forever: your personality. However, the personality is something you have acquired also, like a character part in a play. It can also be disposed of.

We have now discarded all forms of physical identification, as well as what you may have thought of as your enduring spiritual qualities. And your personality, too. Is there anything left? Yes, the eternal, immortal soul that is you. It may be a little difficult at first to imagine that, as a soul, you don't even have integrity, loyalty, or faith. The soul has no possessions, no personality, no name, no qualities. It simply is. The soul does pass through experiences and can recall them, although it doesn't have a storage organ, like a brain, full of memories. Picture an autumn wind. It sweeps through a tree, and a number of leaves separate from their branches and join the wind. They may travel a short or extensive distance, but eventually they flutter to the ground, while the wind moves onward. The leaves may have temporarily indicated the direction and velocity of the wind, given it substance and shape, as it were, but they were neither qualities nor attributes of the wind. So it is with our bodies, talents, and attitudes. They may briefly express an external form and outline for an indwelling soul, yet none of them belong to that ineffable being.

As a soul, we are a calm, still point. We experience action, emotion, physicality; yet we are none of them. We may ride throughout the universe, entering into various forms and dimensions of reality. Yet, while we sample everything, we acquire nothing.

At this point you may be thinking that it's fine to philosophize about our eternal, possession-less soul, but what does that have to do with day-to-day life? You've got bills to pay, a job you're not crazy about, and a number of interpersonal relationships that are far from ideal. What benefit can understanding the nature of your soul bring to the here and now? The benefit is one of perspective: how you view the world and your life.

The most common ways we think of our lives are in terms of having and doing. Let us first look at having. Each day you are bombarded with thousands of offers and enticements to buy a plethora of things. These advertisements are all geared to a mentality of having. Advertisers approach this mentality along different avenues, by playing on your desires, or fears, or ego. For example: if you want to have a beautiful lifestyle, buy this house; if you want to have good health, take these drugs or vitamins; if you want to have the respect and esteem of your neighbors, buy this luxury automobile. The funny thing about having is that we tend to quickly discount the value of those things we already possess. The yearning to have is consistently focused on those things that we have yet to acquire, so there is always an unease and dissatisfaction with our present state. It is a rare person who feels that she has enough. Of course, the acquisitive drive far outstrips our ability to pay for all of the things we crave. Meanwhile, we have a hard time caring for and storing all the stuff we already have.

We are also very concerned with doing. The most important thing we must do is our job, so that we can make the money to pay for all those things we feel compelled to have. There is also the doing that is involved with running and maintaining our household—cleaning, cooking, child-care, etc. Other forms of doing include exercise, socializing, entertainment, travel, and self-improvement. After all, we want to live full lives, and activity is the main trait that distinguishes the quick from the dead.

Now let's return to the soul. Each individual consciousness, be it you or me, is a *being.* It is not a having, nor is it even a doing. You can exist, and do exist, without possessions and without activity. In this world, we tend to define ourselves so much by what we have and what we do that we lose sight of the permanent, effervescent, and happy being that lies buried under all the clutter. In this life we often get so caught up in our possessions and activities that we forget that we **are,** and that being is sufficient unto itself. You can have a lot, a little, or nothing, yet you still are. You can do a lot, a little, or nothing, yet you still are. When we feel overwhelmed by life—put upon, stressed, overworked—we are suffering from an excess of having and doing. We never have too much, nor too little, of being. We simply and always are, and our state of being is always one of sufficiency.

It can be of great benefit each day to reconnect with our fundamental, sufficient state of being. This physical earth is an immense place, and we cannot possess it all. Likewise, the duration of our stay here is a limited one, and we won't have the time to take all the trips we want to, participate in all the activities we would like to, or even attend all the parties to which we are invited. It is common to feel that we do not have enough, and that we do not do enough. However, **we always are enough.**

From time to time, perhaps for a little while each day, it is helpful to put aside the mentality of having and doing. Enter into the simple state of being, and see how the world appears and feels to you when you don't feel that you must possess any portion of it, and you don't have to do anything with it or to it. As a pleasant little exercise, go for a drive in a country area you are not familiar with. The scenery will be new to you, so it won't call up any past associations. You are simply an observer of the passing scene. As you drive along, observe the houses with their lawns and gardens, the farms, barns, and fields. None of it belongs to you, so you are not responsible for paying mortgages or taxes on any of it. You do not have to repair and maintain any of the buildings, nor cut the lawns or weed the gardens. Yet it is all there for you to observe and enjoy. When you engage in *being,* you can appreciate everything in this present moment of its being as it is. If you become a little more adept at this exercise, you can walk into a department store and enjoy the colors and textures, sights and smells of the place without feeling that you must cart any of it home with you.

Appreciation is a remarkable quality. Appreciation implies open acceptance, and is just a whisker removed from love. When you appreciate something, you don't feel compelled to possess it, nor do anything with it or change it in any way. Coming from your own state of being, you are reveling in its state of being. Looked at in this larger framework, our lives in this world are simply a journey of our being, a ride in the country where we can appreciate the sights and sounds and smells and textures of this earth. When the ride in this life is over, we will take nothing tangible or material with us; even the name we bore and the language we spoke will slip away, for our being, already complete, has no need of them.

Since I've mentioned more than once in this text that we are here to refine, polish, and unfold our souls, you may fairly ask how can we enhance and develop something that is already complete and perfect? I don't really know. Even though the soul is complete, and does not grow by a process of accumulation and accretion, the way we would think of a library adding to its collections, it can still progress. We are accustomed to thinking in physical terms, so that when we use the term growth, the inference is that something is becoming bigger, taller, more complex. The soul has no size, and therefore cannot adequately be described using physical terminology. It is outside of the rational, word-grounded mentality altogether, so anything we say about it will be a pale approximation of what it truly is. Yet, between me and you, words are all we have, so we have to limp along and attempt to draw the best picture we can.

To consider how the complete soul can further refine itself, we need to move away from our physically grounded concepts of growth as a process of expansion and accumulation. It may be better to think in terms of intensity. Picture a row of five pink flowers. Down to the molecule, they are all the exact same size and weight. Yet, looking at them from left to right, they vary in coloration from pale to warm to strong to hot to absolutely eye popping. No one flower is bigger or smaller, heavier or lighter than the others, but they do vary considerably in the intensity of their coloration. Perhaps a more personal example would be for you to think of someone you love. When you first met this person, you may have liked him a little. Over time, as you got to know each other better, shared experiences and dreams, your liking turned into loving. And love comes in a whole spectrum of intensities. You can say that you love ice cream, your dog, your job(!?) your spouse, even the movie you saw last night, and in each case you will be referring to a different intensity of feeling. Even with the person who is the love of your life, you will experience fluctuations in the intensity of that love over time. If you just had a disagreement, you still love him or her, but the intensity may have cooled for a while.

Although even this analogy is a flawed approximation, consider that, with experience and wisdom, the soul intensifies. Again, there is no corresponding physical term with which to describe this further growth of the soul. But take heart. There's no fault with you or your understanding; it's due to the limitations of the rational framework, which cannot encompass and codify the larger, non-rational reality. The point to keep in mind is that, somehow, the soul does progress, even though it is already whole and has no need to grow or improve. Beyond what we can know in this dimension, there is an impetus to venture and experience. And there is an ongoing unfoldment and refinement in which we participate and intensify.

At this point, the best I can do is relate the most profound experience of my life to date, and what it revealed to me. For quite a few years I have worked at suspending the internal chatter of my rational faculty, and I have experienced brief periods with no conscious thoughts. There are certain techniques I have developed, which are like turning off the mental switch that powers the thinking process. I have had still moments, whether lying in bed with my eyes closed or walking or working outdoors, where the body functions in a purposeful way without having to direct my actions with any conscious thoughts. In all of these experiences, while the landscape of my mind was a blank slate, it would always be bounded by a formless, yet still apparent, horizon.

On one particular morning, just before I was about to get out of bed, a couple of aimless thoughts were dancing across my consciousness. I shifted into a technique to dispel them, and when I did, it was like a deeper power within my being piggybacked upon my conscious intention. The effect was much more than simply dispelling thought;

the component words and impressions of those thoughts crumbled and disintegrated. I don't even know if the term landscape of the mind could be applied to the state I had entered, because mentality itself had been swept away. This experience went beyond the capacity of words to describe it. I was in a realm with no horizons or boundaries. Words and thoughts were utterly alien. From the impressions I recall, not only had I gone beyond this physical dimension, I had gone beyond death—in the sense that when you depart this life your awareness might still refer back to your experiences and the people you have known in this world. For me, the whole physical dimension disappeared, and along with it, my personality and ego. I knew I was still alive in this world and would be coming back to it. Yet my earthly personality, which I've spent a lifetime seeking to cultivate and improve, was so inconsequential in this realm that it simply faded away. However, my being was in no distress. I felt completely calm and secure, truly at home. What might seem most remarkable is that I had no sensation of going anywhere. I didn't float out of my body, ascend from the Earth, or fly off to the other side of the galaxy. If there was any sense of movement at all, it was of going within, of actually reconnecting with a center that I've carried inside me always. The most remarkable aspect of the whole experience was that, as my nameless consciousness calmly surveyed a scene where there was no object to see or latch onto, I was not alone. From a direction that I can only describe as deeper within my being, there came—an emanation. There was a rhythmic quality to it, like a vibration or pulse. Without words, without manifestation, I knew that this emanation had great knowledge and potency. The emanation was coming toward me, and I was also a part of it, one with it.

This experience lasted for quite some time. And even when I resumed thinking and went about the activities of my day, I retained a sense of clarity and depth that I had never known before. By the next day, these perceptions had been clouded over and obscured with the familiar haze of rational thinking. But for that little while, all thinking, and the accompanying mentalities of having and doing, had completely dissolved. I had returned to a state of pure being and dynamic changelessness, and had I experienced a direct connection with the One which is All.

You may or may not ever slip into an experience this profound during your current lifetime. Be assured that this state of consciousness is accessible to you; it is one in which you exist right now, although it is buried under all of your rational thoughts and attitudes. Be aware that your being existed before this physical planet, solar system, and galaxy came into existence. You can always return to your being-nature, for it is what, at the very core, you are. Having and doing are features of this world that you came here to experience, but keep in mind that they are not intrinsic, essential qualities of existence. We tend to get caught up in desires to have certain things in this world, or to do certain tasks and participate in certain activities. It is all well and good to sample the stuff of this world, intimately involve ourselves in physicality, and engage in all sorts of activities. Just bear in mind that having and doing are dimensions of reality to explore. They are not inherent properties of our being. Revel in the experience of this life, yet know that your soul pervades the entire universe.

Chapter Twenty-Eight
Epilogue

In a book discussing the workings of life on Earth, I have spent much time talking about concepts that extend far beyond this physical realm. The material world, however, is a very small slice of reality; to really understand it, we need to look at how it fits into the larger context of existence. The spiritual dimension surrounds, encloses, and interpenetrates this physical Earth. And while our material bodies move about and display a whole range of living properties, life itself extends far beyond the physical realm. At their core, the issues of life are spiritual issues, so if we really want to get to the heart of what living is all about, we must look at the spiritual.

The three main concepts around which this book has been organized are eternity, divinity, and unity. You are an eternal, divine being, inseparably linked to every other being in one grand, unbreakable Unity of All. As such, you are blessed, worthy, indestructible, and equal to everyone and everything else. As an individuated consciousness, you have a sense of yourself and of other beings existing outside of yourself. The concept of separation is illusory. The illusion has a practical value in that it allows you to engage in individual actions and to reflect on experiences that are unique to your being. But, just like a raindrop bouncing up and down in the topsy-turvy world of a summer thunderstorm, you will eventually land in the sea and contribute your experiences to the grand, all-encompassing identity of the one ocean.

We have looked at the linear nature of rational thought, and at how this one-dimensional thinking process splits the unified world into sets of opposing qualities. We need to think in order to evaluate alternatives and make decisions, but overusing our rationality usually gives us a skewed view of the world and leads to arguments and anguish. It is good to remind yourself at least several times each day that thinking is only one way of apprehending the world, and a very limited one at that. Be aware of the polar nature of your thoughts and seek out moments when you can experience the world in a three-dimensional manner, without thinking.

Remember that everything moves in cycles and spirals. You are going to have your ups and downs. That is the natural flow and movement of life. It is folly to think you can, or should, be happy all the time. Nobody arrives at a plateau, where he has all his problems solved and will never face difficulty again. Each moment is a fresh start, a new opportunity to be positive or negative, to cooperate or find fault. This world is dynamic and inexhaustible; there will always be new challenges, and new wonders beckoning us onward.

In every person, animal, and thing you encounter, you are meeting another manifestation of Divine Oneness. You can learn something from every relationship and interaction. Above all, you are always being invited to respond with love. When you bestow your affection and kindness on others, you are also expanding and ennobling yourself.

Enjoy this life, even in its painful and difficult moments. You are here for the ride. While your body may become bruised, and you may also undergo a great deal of stress and psychological turmoil, keep in mind that underneath the physical surface you are perpetually unscathed, whole, and safe. Take relish in living each day. Smile at adversity, laugh at misfortune. Remember that you are like an actor in a play, performing a role. The day will come when you will step off the stage of this world, remove the costume of your body, and wash off the makeup of your acquired ego and personality. While you're here, get your money's worth out of the stage, the sets, your costume and makeup, and all of the other marvelous actors with whom you have been fortunate to interact. Play your part for all you're worth. Make the living of your life a grand, award-winning performance. You truly are a star. The more you allow your inner radiance to shine forth, the more spectacular and en-lightened the production of this universe will be.

www.ingramcontent.com/pod-product-compliance
Lightning Source LLC
Chambersburg PA
CBHW021050090426
42738CB00006B/266